A New World of Writers

AC / SS — Adolescent Cultures, School & Society

Joseph L. DeVitis & Linda Irwin-DeVitis
General Editors

Vol. 21

PETER LANG
New York • Washington, D.C./Baltimore • Bern
Frankfurt am Main • Berlin • Brussels • Vienna • Oxford

Elaine Freedman Fredericksen

A New World of Writers

Teaching Writing in a Diverse Society

PETER LANG
New York • Washington, D.C./Baltimore • Bern
Frankfurt am Main • Berlin • Brussels • Vienna • Oxford

Library of Congress Cataloging-in-Publication Data

Fredericksen, Elaine Freedman.
A new world of writers: teaching writing
in a diverse society / Elaine Freedman Fredericksen.
p. cm. — (Adolescent cultures, school and society; vol. 21)
Includes bibliographical references and index.
1. Minorities—Education (Secondary)—United States. 2. Language
arts (Secondary)—United States. I. Title. II. Adolescent
cultures, school & society; vol. 21.
LC3731 .F715   808'.042'071273—dc21   00-066415
ISBN 0-8204-5500-8
ISSN 1091-1464

Die Deutsche Bibliothek-CIP-Einheitsaufnahme

Fredericksen, Elaine Freedman:
A new world of writers: teaching writing
in a diverse society / Elaine Freedman Fredericksen.
-New York; Washington, D.C./Baltimore; Bern;
Frankfurt am Main; Berlin; Brussels; Vienna; Oxford: Lang.
(Adolescent cultures, school and society; Vol. 21)
ISBN 0-8204-5500-8

Cover design by Joni Holst

The paper in this book meets the guidelines for permanence and durability
of the Committee on Production Guidelines for Book Longevity
of the Council of Library Resources.

© 2003 Peter Lang Publishing, Inc., New York
275 Seventh Avenue, 28th Floor, New York, NY 10001
www.peterlangusa.com

Printed in the United States of America

TABLE OF CONTENTS

ACKNOWLEDGMENTS

I would like to thank The University of Texas at El Paso, particularly the Department of English, for supporting and encouraging my research. Thanks also to my students who have so generously submitted to my experimental pedagogy, and who have given me permission to use their writing as part of my scholarship. Their voices enhance the text in a very special way.

Much of what I know about teaching has come to me through observation, conversation, and lore. If I have had any individual epiphanies, they have been products of what others have led me to understand. For this legacy, I thank my teachers and colleagues, too numerous to name but gratefully remembered.

I could not have finished this volume without the able assistance of Sonya Saunders, my technical assistant, and editor, Joseph DeVitis.

Special thanks to Sandy Krist for personal encouragement and advice when my brain refused to work.

Finally, to Tony Stafford, my helpmate.

INTRODUCTION
Learning to Teach in a Diverse Society

Teachers used to know what to expect on the first day of class. They had a good notion of what their students would look like, what language they would speak, and what their backgrounds and expectations would be. Teachers also knew what to teach; their job was to pass on the same traditional truths they had learned during their own schooling to students who would receive them eagerly—or at least without overt protest. However, the faces of American students have changed. Anyone currently teaching, particularly at the secondary level, recognizes that in many neighborhoods, students once labeled "minorities" (Hispanic, black, Asian, lower-class, disabled) now often outnumber so-called "traditional" white middle-class students. Unfortunately, although individual teachers or faculties have worked hard to adapt their own instruction, teaching methodology in general has not changed as rapidly as student population, and the old methods have not always met the needs of diverse student learners.

A New World of Writers is directed toward teachers, school administrators, and parents of adolescents in the new century. Focusing particularly on writing as a path to educational success, each chapter of this book takes a look at a specific segment of the new school population or at a specific problem encountered by nontraditional students. The author then offers practical solutions to the problems, based on current theory.

The majority of secondary and early postsecondary students used to be preteens or teenagers. There were more males than females. More came from middle-class than lower-class families. White students far outnumbered ethnic and racial minorities except in certain neighborhoods, often in large cities, where almost all students were people of color; these schools were not considered desirable places of employment for the average white teacher. Most students at all schools spoke English as a first language; those who did not were usually relegated to "special" or "remedial" classes that also served youngsters with behavioral or developmental problems as well as those with physical disabilities. Such classes tended to be few and small and were staffed by a small, hearty band of special education teachers.

United States Census statistics reveal how much student populations now differ from the former norm. The Census Bureau's 1999 Current Population Survey lists the total U.S. school enrollment at 57,191,000. In high schools, the survey counted 2,536,000 African Americans, 2,290,000 Hispanic Americans, and 719,000 Asian Americans. College enrollments included 1,998,000 African Americans, 1,307,000 Hispanic Americans, and 1,042,000 Asian Americans. These numbers do not include recent immigrants. A 2001 *Washington Post* article, "For Immigrant Kids: A World of Struggle" from Tuesday, May 29, 2001, claims that "one of every five students in U.S. schools is an immigrant," and "80% of those are students of color. In two generations, nearly half the population will be people of color and the children and grandchildren of today's immigrants." Another element in the student mix is a growing population of students with identified disabilities— either physical or cognitive. Once isolated from the mainstream and taught by specially trained educators, these young people now attend regular classes but require various accommodations to maximize success.

This changing student population brings a welcome diversity to the school system, but it also promises a variety of unwelcome problems for educators trained in traditional methodology. Students are changing, but most teachers still represent white, middle-class attitudes and values. Surveys of teacher education programs in the United States indicate that many new teachers—most of whom are white, middle-class women—leave school and enter their own classrooms unprepared for the diversity they will meet. They will surely face unexpected frustrations and, unless change occurs, there will be an ever-increasing gap between what students need and what teachers are prepared to deliver.

This problem has not gone unnoticed. Teaching methodology has changed considerably since the 1960s, with important movement toward student-centered classrooms, collaborative learning, individualized instruction, and extracurricular activity. In writing classes, outcomes now focus on a process motivated by social and cultural situations rather than on a single final product. Still, pedagogy lags behind the tremendous population shift. This book argues for further transformation designed to meet the multiple needs of students in a diverse and mobile society. It is an idealistic proposal based on the notion that articulated goals produce better results than unarticulated ones. Progress in education never occurs quickly, but progress is possible.

Chapter One of this text confronts the complex and difficult issue of difference, particularly in an educational system where most teachers are white and most students are people of color. It argues that white educators must acknowledge that their own race matters just as much as the races and ethnicities of their students. White skin and white standards have been accepted as the invisible norm by which students are measured, but this paradigm no longer matches reality in most American classrooms. Rather than continuing to expect students to adjust, teachers can learn to see their students as they really are. They can forego the "us-them" binary and join with their students in an effort to create new knowledge together.

Chapter Two, reprinted from an article in *Language Arts*, examines the problem of gender difference and shows how girls and young women may be silenced or ignored by a traditional educational system. It offers available methods for equalizing opportunities for females and males and for helping female students find their classroom voices.

Chapter Three reports on an experiment with collaborative learning communities in a mainly Mexican American university setting. This report suggests that collaborative methods can work well with this particular group of students and that it is worth trying with other traditionally marginalized groups.

Chapter Four discusses negotiated grading as an empowering methodology for young writers. Because most students have learned to write for a grade, they aim to please the teacher. Negotiated grading teaches them to reflect on their own writing processes and to evaluate their own product. Through this method, they begin to think of themselves as writers rather than as students who are being forced to write. This attitudinal shift is important for students who buy into the stereotype that minority students cannot be successful in classes that include a writing component.

Chapter Five tackles the problem of academic authority in student writing. It suggests a method for moving students from personal to public expression and a gradual acquisition of the conventions of academic writing. Student samples model the process from free-writing through finished documented essay.

Chapter Six encourages teachers to create a playful atmosphere in the classroom. It shows how simulations and games can build community and alleviate fear. Purposeful play does not waste time; it helps students learn through doing and teaches them that learning can be fun.

Chapter Seven forefronts an often invisible minority population— students with physical and learning disabilities. Using theory and common sense, educators can help these students become an integral part of the classroom community adding an important layer to the issue of diversity—students with various levels of ability can teach others at the same time they learn.

This book is an attempt to present a clearer picture of today's students and teachers. It brings together divergent educational theories and years of lore. The result is a series of observations and suggestions offered in the hope that they will interest, inform, and perhaps inspire those hardworking teachers engaged in the very difficult task of educating the multifaceted students of the twenty-first century.

CHAPTER ONE
Shapeshifters: Adapting to a New Tradition in Writing Instruction

In any one of the classes I teach, I may be the only member who is not a person of color. Usually I am the only person in the classroom over forty and, on many occasions, the only one over thirty. Some of my students consider themselves middle class like me, but many do not.

Although I am small in stature, friendly, and student-centered, my students say they find me intimidating. "Why?" I ask them. "It's the way you look," they say, "the way you talk." What they mean is that I am different, not like them. In fact, very few teachers are young people of color. Instead, most are quite a bit like me: white, articulate native English speakers, middle class, older than their students, and perplexed about how to do an effective job with today's population of nontraditional students. Teachers complain that students seem less prepared for school each year, less eager to engage in the subject matter, less willing to write. Students may, either actively or passively, resist assimilation, reject reading materials that do not seem to apply to their home culture, and resent standards set by a dominant white authority. An apparent solution to this problem is to hire more teachers from diverse cultures, but this solution is not practical. Although numbers have increased slightly in recent years, still only a relatively small percentage of minority students enter institutions of higher learning; even fewer aspire to the teaching profession. This means that in the foreseeable future, teachers will continue to look, act, speak, and feel very different from their students. They will have different goals and expectations. A failure to address the major gaps between teachers and students portends trouble in twenty-first—century classrooms.

Educators dedicated to transformation and reform must recognize that social theories of personal identity have come into conflict with outdated educational theories of schools as perpetuators of American one-standard-for-all democracy. The time has come to recognize that traditional pedagogy, although it may have produced satisfactory results in the past, no longer serves the majority of American students.

Conflicting Theories

As early as 1934, social psychologist George H. Mead expressed concern about identity, how it was formed, and what it implied. Mead believed that humans were differentiated from animals because they possessed a sense of self that "is not initially there at birth, but arises in the process of social experience and activity, that is, develops in the given individual as a result of his [her] relations to the process as a whole and to other individuals within the process" (135). Thus, humans develop a unique identity based on the culture that surrounds them: their parents, institutions, climate, local customs, and other cultural variables. Perhaps the most important of these is language, the major vehicle by which cultural knowledge is conveyed. If Mead is correct, an immigrant student from Laos or Cambodia will have an entirely different sense of self—a different identity—from a native, and an African American student will have a self-concept different from that of her Latin American classmate or her white teacher. Certainly they will share some aspects of identity, but much will differ. They may all know and use English, but they will not speak the same social language. This creates problems in schools developed on century-old educational theory.

From the beginnings of American education, theorists linked education and democracy. They felt that classrooms should mirror society and teach young people to become good citizens. In 1921, John Dewey saw education as both national and social (108) and defined democracy as a "mode of associated living, a conjoint communicated experience" (101). These ideas are echoed by Joseph Tussman who said in 1969 that college should "prepare successive generations to carry on and develop the life of the culture" (24). These theories work well if we assume the nation is a single culture and if the major goal of immigrants and subcultures is to assimilate, to become part of mainstream America. Unfortunately, in America today, minority populations have come to realize that all the time in the world may not allow them to share equally in the benefits of the American dream. Although individual members of minority communities have achieved fame or riches or both, as a whole, nonwhites still outnumber whites in America's lower classes, still are less likely to graduate from high school or enter post-secondary educational institutions, still have much higher attrition rates when they do attend colleges and universities, and still do not feel accepted on the same level as whites.

Because hundreds of years of effort and patience have not brought equality to native-born people of color, they now often resist assimilation and place more value on their particular racial and ethnic identities. The same is true for many new immigrants who seek prosperity, but not a loss of culture. These students do not want an education that tries to change who they are. They want an education that values their differences and that recognizes that white is also a race. People of color in this country know intuitively and empirically what many whites cannot or will not acknowledge—that race is about power, not about skin color. More and more, minority Americans reject as elitist the notion of a single culture. They know that the norms of standard English and academic voice reflect white culture, not their own. This rejection places white teachers on very shaky ground.

Of course, education pedagogy has undergone considerable change since the 1960s. James Berlin reports in *A Short History of Writing Instruction* on the shift toward cultural awareness which has led educators (including Britton, Berthoff, Graves, Macrorie, Shaughnessy, Emig, and others) to make "writing instruction sensitive to the social dimensions of learning and writing, particularly in issues of class, race, and gender" (216). There has been increased interest in the social nature of learning, an idea introduced by educational psychologist Lev Vygotsky early in the 1900s and revisited by modern theorists like Michael Cole and Barbara Rogoff. It has been only very recently that theorists have focused on the pedagogical implications of race and turned their attentions to the problematic notion of teacher position.

Curtis Branch notes how teachers' attitudes and behaviors can influence a youngster's developing sense of identity through curriculum choices, responses to diversity, and through "the perceptions of power distance and how it creates a sense of marginality and devaluation" (23). When educational theorists promote democratic schools, they often argue for a color-blind approach wherein each student gets the same treatment, reads the same material, and adheres to the same standards. This idealistic program does not function as planned in a less-than-ideal society. In fact, this so-called democratic plan has been created and administered by middle-class whites. Its standards are white standards, and its power base favors homes where standard English is spoken. It does not adequately take into consideration the developing racial and ethnic identities of nonwhite students or make allowances for their special needs or interests. Teachers have tried to be more inclusive by adding writers of color to reading lists, but this is not sufficient.

Even well-intentioned efforts by people of color can backfire when they are isolated and not carefully considered. Todd DeStigter reports, for example, on the activities planned by the Multicultural Awareness Club at a predominately white high school. The idea was to introduce students to Black History Month and Cinco de Mayo by inviting guest speakers and serving ethnic foods. Unfortunately, the dishes presented as representative— barbecued ribs, fried chicken, greens for Black History and tacos, beans, and rice for Cinco de Mayo—inadvertently perpetuated stereotypes and further marginalized African American and Latino students. In this instance, as DeStigter explains, "The very people the dominant oppresses are contributing to their own subjugation" (219).

Sporadic efforts at enlightenment have had little lasting effect. Real transformation will take place only when educators examine their own racial, ethnic, gender, and class identities and when they recognize how often middle-class white standards are imposed on lower-class nonwhite students. Today's diverse student population requires a wider educational vision that fits the needs and capabilities of a broad range of learners; teachers need to assess their own position and be willing to adjust their attitudes and teaching styles to fit their students rather than expecting students to adapt to them.

To do this, educators can develop new methods that stress "the constant undermining, on the part of both professors and students, of fixed essential identities" (Gibson et al., 69). This requires repeated, direct confrontation of issues of race, ethnicity, gender, and class. Henry Giroux sees this approach as a quest for a new kind of democratic education in which students and teachers work together to transform society. Transformation remains elusive, however, when educators refuse to see themselves clearly, to accept that white is also a race, or to acknowledge the difficulties inherent in a system where older, richer, whiter people set standards that younger, poorer, less-educated people of color must meet to succeed. Conversely, new teaching methods can achieve success in mixed classrooms when white teachers are willing to examine, discuss, and resolve the weighty issue of their own race and its implications for classroom power distribution. "In order for teachers to promote a healthy identity for themselves and their pupils," argues Etta Hollins, "they must begin with self-understanding" (192). This will happen when Americans—and particularly American teachers—acknowledge that white is a race. It is not invisible, and it does make a difference in classroom power balances.

Defining Race

White educators—and whites in general—have had problems seeing themselves as "raced," perhaps because the very definition of race remains elusive. Branch defines race as "a concept that is derived from a genetic designation based on phenotypic characteristics (i.e., physical features such as skin color and hair texture)" (7), but the term is often confused with ethnicity. Furthermore, he points out that "race, as a category, may subsume several ethnic groups and in doing so, obliterates any uniqueness associated with more narrowly defined ethnic categories" (7). In order to understand the complexity of race and ethnicity, one need merely consider the differences between a black-skinned person from Puerto Rico and one from South Africa. They come from different countries, speak different languages, have different religious beliefs, and eat different foods. Obviously they share little more than the color of their skin. Yet definitions of race link them more closely than, for example, a Mexican American and African American living next door to one another on a street in Los Angeles, California, and attending the same high school.

Although the debate continues over what designates race and how it may be distinguished from ethnicity, many white people dismiss the question as a nonissue. To most whites, race means anybody different from them, anybody nonwhite, anybody "other." Whites tend to take their own biology for granted because it affects their lives mainly in positive ways. They are more likely to receive privileges based on their skin color than to be denied them. This does not hold true for people of color who often lose privilege because of their biological makeup. Thus, questions of race become questions of power. Timothy Barnett believes that "race is not a function of biology but a construct of language and culture" (15). He argues that whiteness is not invisible, as many whites believe; rather it visually marks power over "a large body of 'others' who are not white" (10). Race becomes important to educators when it mixes with power dynamics because students who feel powerless do not learn as well as those who feel empowered. They also react against those in power when they feel threatened. Teachers traditionally wield the power in the classroom, but most attempt to provide their students with a certain degree of autonomy. When they do this successfully, students like their classes and perform well. Sharing power becomes more difficult, however, when the teacher is the only white person in the class because students of color know where they stand in society; they know that white skin means strength. So when they enter a white teacher's classroom, they receive a double whammy. If the teacher ignores the imbalance, students are likely to resist, and resistance impedes learning.

White Matters

Once during my first student teaching experience, I told my training teacher that the students did not really see me. "They're so involved in themselves and each other," I complained. "They hardly know I'm here."

"They see you," that wise man assured me.

So I put it to the test. The next day I wore two different colored shoes—not a blatant black and white contrast, but a more subtle navy blue on the right foot, black on the left. Nearly every student noticed and commented on the discrepancy. From this experience, I learned that students are far more observant and interested than teachers give them credit for. They see us.

Many of my fellow teachers refuse to acknowledge this. They insist that their students do not notice their skin color. They get annoyed with me when I bring up the subject of race, which they consider unimportant as long as they treat everyone equally. Then I hear these same colleagues lamenting the poor preparation of their students or their poor use of language. They complain that students do not read at home or that they never look at a newspaper. Teachers don't like the way their students speak out in class—or refuse to speak up. In other words, they are keyed into the various cultural and language differences of their students at the same time they disregard their own. They honestly do not understand how much they rely on traditional white values and how impossible it is for many students of color to meet those standards.

I believe that much classroom discord and discomfort, and a good deal of teacher dissatisfaction, has to do with tradition and power. As Chris Weedon reminds us, "in mainstream discourse of race, whiteness functions as an unmarked neutral category, a norm which is the equivalent of being human." Weedon is concerned about society's refusal to recognize "the status of whiteness as a socially and historically changing construct and its role in the perpetuation of racist assumptions" (154). Teachers have been taught to view minority students as "other" and to make allowances for minority students' inability to catch on quickly or to keep up, or to speak our language properly. We have not been taught to question our own inability to speak their languages (Spanish, Chinese, Korean, Vietnamese, or whatever) or to catch up on their cultures or personal awareness. We learn to accept the various skin colors of our students, but we have not been reminded that they must also accept ours. Certainly, no one tells us that students see *us* as "other" or that often they resent our position of power. In fact, "very few teachers admit to believing in white superiority, although there may be evidence of such in their classroom practices" (Hollins, 185).

"I treat everyone fairly," most teachers will exclaim, and, indeed, they make every effort to do this. They fail, however, to recognize how much the standards applied in the classroom are white standards. What language do we teach? White Standard American. On what culture are our examinations based? White Standard American. Ian Marshall and Wendy Ryden warn that "Whites, while making their own whiteness invisible, but not inconsequential, reproduce the values, culture, and language of the elite" (241). They may do so unwittingly, avoiding questions about race because it seems insignificant to them or because students seem reluctant to discuss this subject; however, whether the teacher recognizes it or not, students of color may have a harder time trusting white teachers, and a lack of trust upsets the learning environment.

Rosa Hernandez Sheets reports on her experiences with a class of at-risk ninth graders where "all of the ethnic students of color made negative comments about white teachers in general, about particular white teachers, and about white peers" (161). This suggests that students see and care about racial difference and that sometimes they will respond in negative ways to white teachers and classmates merely because of their skin color. These bad feelings can cloud the classroom atmosphere and make it harder for students to learn. They can also make teachers feel uneasy, unproductive, and frustrated. Bringing negative feelings into the open and discussing them can clear the air and improve the learning environment.

Teachers generally recognize how much home culture impacts student learning, but often use this recognition to blame families for students' school failures. Instead of placing blame on the home culture, teachers "may want to think seriously about the identities we bring with us into the classroom, remain conscious of the way those identities interact with the identities our students bring and insert ourselves fully into the shifting relationships between ourselves and our students at the same time that we resist the impulse to control those relationships" (Gibson et al., 92—3). In other words, educators can look at and capitalize on the knowledge and abilities students bring to the classroom. We can find greater success by working with and through a multicultural lens rather than by viewing the world from an exclusively white perspective.

Can the problem of racial difference between teacher and students be resolved? Can white teachers teach nonwhite students about whiteness when they hardly think about it themselves? Even if they work hard to think about it, what language will they use to discuss it when no language has existed before? According to Marshall and Ryden, students need a "genuine invitation" to dialogue or they may resist discussing race. Multicultural artifacts like Cisneros's short stories or photographs of Africa do little good unless teacher and students can have honest, open discussions with teacher and students ready to listen as well as speak. In the course of discussion, issues of power and race can be aired. The teacher may want more cooperation; students may want a stronger voice, more decision-making power. They may feel they have no power because they are not white. This dialogue and its direct confrontation of race has to be addressed on a continuing daily basis, not as a one-time attempt. Race does not come and go; it is constant. It always matters.

Of course, difference is not simply a matter of race. Students also bring to school myriad ethnic, class, religious, gender, health, and language traits. Teachers in many geographic areas consider themselves fortunate if only two languages are native to their students. Many large-city class populations encompass five, ten, or even more different language groups. Any given class can also include Christian, Jewish, and Muslim worshippers. It can include heterosexual and homosexual students; students with widely ranging physical and mental abilities; rich, middle-class, and poor students. Parents and society at large expect teachers to blend these ingredients into a workable stew—a happy, active, productive classroom where everyone learns and no one feels alienated. Even teachers who care deeply about their students, who value cross-cultural understanding, who promote social reform and resist oppression need help in addressing the complex makeup of today's nontraditional audience.

The Teacher's Place in the Classroom

Elizabeth Ellsworth describes the difficulty of teaching in classrooms that encompass a wide range of cultures and values. She says that students may seem to have "a passion for ignorance" (57), an active refusal to learn that stems from their resistance to a teacher and a system designed to make them conform and assimilate. She says we need to seek a new student-teacher relationship that remains in flux rather than being fixed. Her suggestion for dealing with poor communication between a teacher and students is to make teaching "a suspended performance in the sense that it is never completed or finished. And it is suspended in the sense that we, as teachers, must stop ourselves if students are to take on responsibility for the meanings they make" (158). Thus, teachers must frequently step away from the front of the classroom and cede center stage to the students, particularly in areas where students have greater knowledge (as in discussions of literature based on the students', and not the teachers', culture). When teachers give due credit to the knowledge students bring to the classroom, students are more likely to admit that perhaps the teacher knows something too.

This sounds like an easy solution, but, of course, it goes against tradition in multiple ways. Even educators who aim for student-centered classrooms believe that teachers have to select and supervise activities, present standards, assign grades, and assure that all students address and profit from the district or institution-directed curriculum. For traditional educators, administrators, and parents, lack of teacher authority spells chaos.

Traditionally oriented educators generally expect students and their families to adapt to the school system, making whatever changes seem necessary to allow youngsters to fit in and perform to standard. Unfortunately, the system tends to overlook the feelings of nontraditional students. Stephen Brown describes marginalized students entering the classroom and "experiencing a violent rupture with their home culture and an equally violent 'initiation' into the dominant culture" (53). As representatives of that dominant group, white teachers simply cannot conduct business as usual. They must recognize and find ways to address the "shock, uncertainty, insecurity, alienation, confusion, and homesickness" (Brown, 54) these students carry to school more ubiquitously than their book-laden backpacks.

What do these students need that traditional methodology does not provide? They need a way to acknowledge the differences between themselves and the teacher as well as those between their individual selves and those of their fellow students. They need a venue for discussing these differences. Most importantly, they need tools to resist the power imbalances inherent in the traditional system and permission to wield these tools.

According to Henry A. Giroux, a leading proponent of critical pedagogy, a multicultural approach to education can help today's students if this approach affirms "cultural differences while simultaneously refusing to essentialize and grant immunity to those groups that speak from subordinate positions of power" (236). This means that white educators must not categorize minority students as poor, undereducated people who need special treatment. Rather the educators should seek a curriculum and methodology that encompasses the interests and talents of many different learners. They must acknowledge the power imbalances that exist within any classroom—those between teacher and student and those among students—and confront rather than ignore these distributions. Students need a space to voice their concerns and objections. They need to be able to say, "That's not fair." They deserve an opportunity to make choices about what they read and write, and they deserve an open-minded, unbiased reading. A white teacher who refuses to recognize that white is a race, and that race matters very much, cannot hope to provide the optimal learning environment for students of color. So one essential shift required of teachers is that which moves them from a color-blind world toward a multicolor one. Or to use a common metaphor, white educators need to remove the lenses they have been looking through, the ones that see students as they used to be—homogeneous, white, middle class, and eager to replicate the value system of their teachers. Instead they must learn to see their students clearly, to attempt to learn who they really are and how they feel.

The New-Traditional Classroom: An Ideal Vision

What would an ideal classroom look like? I see it as a comfortable, non-hierarchical, noncompetitive safe space where students and teacher, regardless of difference, work together toward common goals. I see busy group work interspersed with mini-lessons presented either by the teacher or by individual students or groups of students. I see assessment based on communally developed rubrics. I see grades negotiated between teacher and student. I see growth as students and teachers share and create knowledge, learning together.

How would such a classroom sound? I hear conversation, laughter, debate. I hear an occasional argument that ends without either consensus or acrimony. I hear mutual respect and a willingness to express opinions without fear of censure. I hear the voice of reason.

Totally unrealistic? Partially, perhaps, but not totally. I know from years of teaching at all levels with different populations in various parts of two countries how most real classrooms usually look and sound. I know about standardized testing, school regulations, discipline problems, violence, apathy, parental neglect, low pay, long hours, and too many papers to grade. But I also know that even when an ideal may be difficult or impossible to achieve, it still helps to articulate that ideal. Humans need goals to work toward and the promise of something better to come. Not everyone will approach a particular goal in the same way. Every situation, every group of participants is unique. Still, educators share a desire to teach. We seek a methodology that creates learning and an environment in which students can profit from the method. So this book sets forth an ideal for all of us, along with some tentative suggestions for a new pedagogy suited to today's diverse learners.

The basic precepts of this pedagogy are idealistic but achievable in small increments. All any teacher can do is work within the given set of circumstances, keeping one eye on the lofty goal and another on the rambunctious students, implementing gradual changes and testing their effectiveness before making adjustments and moving on. The changes I suggest are the following, made in full realization that they will not work for everyone but in the hope that teachers will try them out:

(1) Rethink the teacher's place in the classroom and make a real effort to cede center stage to the students.
(2) Allow students power over their own knowledge and determine to learn from your students at the same time you offer what you know.
(3) Do your best to know and enjoy the students' home communities.
(4) Create a classroom atmosphere that welcomes discussion and confrontation, accepting that consensus is not the necessary outcome of conflict and the dialogue can be more valuable than resolution.

Shared Authority

In the ideal classroom, teachers share power with students. Of course, the trained adults have responsibility for maintaining order, keeping records, writing grades on report cards, and planning overall learning goals. But students provide input to make learning more meaningful to them. They work together with the teacher to formulate specific classroom goals and rules for behavior. They skim required texts early in the school year or semester and vote for readings they prefer to concentrate on. They contribute outside materials—books from home, favorite poems or song lyrics, newspaper or magazine articles—and these, too, become part of the curriculum.

Even in traditional schools, teachers generally have enough latitude to take some chances with curriculum and the canon. Within given parameters, and while continuing to work toward convincing administrators to widen those parameters, they can give students some choices. Youngsters need a chance to say, "I can't read this stuff. Can't we see the movie?" Of course, this does not mean that a teacher should substitute films for reading, but it may be a signal for the teacher to read some of the text aloud until students are engaged. Or students may be ready to accept assigned roles and prepare to act out a scene or two from a literary work. When students must remain silent, bowing to the teacher's constant authority, they do not feel free to voice their frustrations and remain, without the teacher's awareness, barred from entering the world of the text. By contrast, students who choose materials and help set class objectives generally read the texts and strive to meet the goals because all seem relevant to their needs and interests.

Students also do better if they write from their own experiences rather than from the experiences of a teacher who, more often than not, is totally different from them. Traditional teachers tend to stick to the text and ask students to write about the text, but if famous directors can set Romeo and Juliet in the modern era, why can't students recast literature with their friends and move the setting to their own neighborhoods? Why can't they use rap rhythms and home language in their narratives? Applying adult, white, middle-class standards to young people of color and of other classes makes no sense. These standards silence students rather than giving them voice. Students need latitude, a room for creativity, and deferral of hierarchical standards until their creative work is done. Then they can proofread, edit, and revise with the help of teacher and peers.

Students can help with methodology, too. They can learn to evaluate their own writing based on a rubric or set of guidelines that they decide upon communally. They can choose when to do peer reviews and let teachers know when they prefer teacher comments. They can work in groups to devise test questions, and they can brainstorm appropriate writing topics that revolve around their communities, their lives, and their personal concerns. All of these activities make students feel like planners rather than followers. These kinds of choices actually relieve teachers of some of their duties, thus freeing them to concentrate on other areas like taking more time to comment on student work or engaging in individual conferences with students.

Traditional teachers like to be in front of the classroom, with all eyes facing them. This promotes hierarchical thinking and hinders creativity. When teachers step aside, when they promote group work and student leadership, students tend to become more actively engaged in class activities. If teachers circulate to listen in on collaborative discussions rather than dominating every conversation, their students come to see them as coaches and facilitators rather than as dictators. This strengthens students' self-confidence and helps them appreciate rather than fear the teacher. In many ways, shared authority encourages learning.

What Students Know

Too often, educators think they have all the answers. They see their job as relaying centuries-old information to uneducated youngsters. What they may fail to recognize is that students bring to class many kinds of knowledge that teachers lack. Each individual tends to know his or her own community, subject field, writing style, and language. In the early days of education, teachers had a good chance of sharing some of these in common with students, but in today's diverse society, difference seems more likely than similarity. Students offer the best opportunity for teachers to learn about other cultures, other neighborhoods, and other languages. But to take advantage of this opportunity, teachers need to recognize how much their students bring to class, and they need to make shared knowledge an important part of daily classroom life.

These sharing skills do not come naturally. We tend to teach the way we learned; we replicate the actions of our own teachers. But teachers can learn to change. Helen Duffy reports on her experience as a teacher educator trying to mentor a student teacher named Deborah. Deborah reported problems with a particular African American student, Jack, who refused to accept her authority. In her selection of readings from Malcolm X, she hoped to interest her students of color, but she failed to realize that she could not present herself, a white woman, as someone who knew more about the motivations of Malcolm X than Jack did. She had to learn, with the help of her mentor, to give Jack the benefit of his knowledge. She had to begin listening to him and her other students. She had to learn from them before they would accept her. She had to respect them before they would respect her and value their voices before they would value what she had to say.

An article by Margaret J. Johnson and Kathryn Button reports on a study of teachers who decided to enroll in a graduate course and, through their own experiences as learners, came to see how much they shared with their elementary students. As the teachers became empowered by what they were learning, they saw that their students also had, and deserved, power. One student-teacher commented, "I chose what I wanted to study and write about. Why not let the kids choose what they want to write about?" She learned to step back from the teacher role and let students teach one another. Engaged in the learning process herself, she came to see her students as learners and knowers. Teachers in this study also learned the importance of meaningful, purposeful assignments. They wanted what they studied to mean something, and they came to understand that their students had the same desire. All of this tells us that good teaching can be learned, that behavior can change. Although teachers must adhere to district standards, they need not be stuck in a traditional model that no longer serves their nontraditional students.

Knowing Our Students

In El Paso, Texas, where I live and teach, many students literally cross an international border every day to attend classes. To serve them and other culturally diverse students, teachers also need to become border crossers, if only in the metaphorical sense. We need, as Giroux suggests, "to explore zones of cultural difference by moving in and out of the resources, histories, and narratives that provide different students with a sense of identity, place, and possibility" (252). In a way, I am very fortunate. I can park my car in downtown El Paso and walk across the bridge into another country. I can hear the language most of my students speak, eat their typical foods, shop in the *mercados* where they shop. While I am there, I can imagine myself in their place and guess how they must feel as they enter the United States each day: *I am uncertain about what people are saying around me; I speak Spanish, but it is not my native tongue; I make mistakes. I do not know my way around, yet hesitate to ask directions; maybe I won't understand the directions I am given. I don't know the laws of this country or the mores of this society. I like it here, but I feel overwhelmed by my own ignorance. Speaking textbook Spanish, dressed in American clothes, unable to mask the whiteness of my skin, I don't fit in. I never will.* Many of my students must have some of these same feelings when they enter my classroom. How can I help allay their fears, provide them opportunities to ask their questions, let them know that I recognize and value their differences?

Most teachers cannot get close to their students' native culture. We cannot travel to Indonesia, China, Romania, Korea, El Salvador, Puerto Rico, Africa, and even if we could visit their homelands, as I do when I cross the bridge into Mexico, we will not really know their culture. We will necessarily remain spectators. If we do happen to know one of their cultures well, there are still many others about which we know virtually nothing. What can be done? Giroux suggests that teachers bear a burden of responsibility for creating bridges among communities. He says teachers cannot just pack up at the end of the school day and head home to a life of power and comfort, but, instead, should educate themselves and, even more, "refigure relations between the school, teachers, students, and the wider community" (251). This means taking part in activities of the school neighborhoods and working to open communications with families of students and with important members of their society. It also means listening to what students, parents, and community leaders say and acting on it, perhaps by making curricular changes that involve decentralization and getting out from under the shadow of standardized tests. In other words, Giroux believes teachers must take political action.

This advice will seem unworkable to overtired teachers at the end of a long school day or week. It will also seem impractical when faced with the realities of a conservative school board or administration, but it can still help us if we take Giroux as the ideal and make small steps within our means. We can certainly invite parents to visit our classrooms, perhaps as guest speakers on a panel or as observers of student performances. Many parents will be unavailable during school hours, but we can send home class publications of student writing. We can, on occasion, attend neighborhood celebrations—street festivals, art shows, parades. We can visit our students' churches if we plan to worship anyway or eat in local restaurants. Then we can talk to our students about these experiences to let them know that we appreciate their community and want to be a part of it.

Even though we may not be naturally interested in politics, we can make an effort to talk about political issues with our students. When they choose writing topics, we can steer them toward local, state, and national issues that impact their lives and their communities. Then, as we read the papers they produce, we will also become more interested and informed.

An individual teacher cannot do everything, but each of us can do something, and whatever we do will be appreciated by our students.

My students tend to avoid conflict. So do I. Harmony feels more comfortable. Unfortunately, harmony is often achieved by a silence that masks underlying problems and promotes passive resistance. Giroux calls harmony "nothing more than an image in the discourse of those who do not have to suffer the injustices experienced by subordinated groups" (126). It is an illusion, fostered by silence, that students do not recognize their relative powerlessness or feel anger at a system that keeps them subservient. Any classroom teacher knows that anger smolders beneath many placid surfaces. It appears disguised in many student behaviors—shouting, slamming books on the desk, shoving, failing to comply with homework assignments, malicious joking, and other forms of acting out. We may assume that the behaviors stem from a bad morning at home or lack of sleep, but perhaps the problem belongs to us, our methods, our system.

We can help our students confront their unspoken resentments by encouraging them to articulate what bothers them. Joe Marshall Hardin suggests that writing classrooms provide an ideal venue for this type of social and political exploration. As students discuss what they read and as they write expressive and argumentative responses, they can bring to light problems in their own lives, in their classrooms, in their school, and in their society.

Certainly many students will initially resist any activities that require confrontation and conflict. Not only do such activities go against previous teaching (Be good. Do what the adult says. Mind your manners. Observe the law.), but they also demand difficult introspection and a willingness to voice unpopular views. Young people have a tremendous desire to fit in with their peers and to receive the teacher's approval. They do not readily take risks. However, teachers can build classroom community before promoting confrontation. Students who already feel safe venture more. Teachers can also promote attitudes of nonjudgmental openness wherein students know that they will not be condemned or ridiculed for expressing opposition. In this atmosphere, students will more willingly confront issues, policies, the teacher, and one another. Such conflict, feared by many, achieves positive results because a problem aired has a much better chance of being solved than one that remains hidden. Furthermore, students trained in confrontation learn to challenge oppression.

All of this must, of course, take place at the same time students practice the course content. Hardin agrees we must teach students standard diction, forms, and other components of academic discourse, but he also thinks we can teach students to "interrogate, critique, and in some cases resist the values promoted by these discourses" (2). He believes young learners can "appropriate and use the rhetoric and conventions of academic and cultural discourses to inscribe their own values" (5). This move is particularly necessary and important to nontraditional students who initially see academic rhetoric as foreign and intimidating. Once they gain control over these linguistic tools, they discover the power language can provide. This is the power they need to succeed as students and citizens.

Tom Fox claims that "the academy is in general hostile to students of color" and that "students of color fail because they are an alienated minority and the victims of overt and covert racism" (77). Fox shows, however, that many African American students succeed when they actively resist white supremacy. To do this, "they do not involve themselves in isolated acts of refusal, but instead ally themselves with traditions of resistance exemplified by historical and contemporary African American intellectuals" (Fox, 71). Teachers at all levels can help African American and other nontraditional students conquer their academic difficulties by providing them with role models, both on paper and in the flesh. They can encourage students to emulate the courage of their heroes by actively confronting an unfriendly system.

White teachers need not stand alone in a classroom filled with nontraditional students. They can enlist adults of color to stand beside them. These adults can be guest speakers, members of the local community, relatives, neighbors, and friends of the students. They can also enter the class in the form of books, CDs, videos, and photographs. White teachers who employ this assistance, who recognize their own difference and discuss it with the class frequently, who try to know their students and plan for their specific needs, and who encourage an atmosphere of productive confrontation will never have to stand alone. Their students will stand with them.

WORKS CITED

Barnett, Timothy. "Reading 'Whiteness' in English Studies." *College English*, 63.1, 9–37, September 2000.

Berlin, James. "Writing Instruction in School and College English, 1890-1985." In *A Short History of Writing Instruction: From Ancient Greece to Twentieth-Century America*. Ed. James J. Murphy. Davis, CA: Hermagoras Press, 1990. 183–220.

Branch, Curtis W. "Race and Human Development." In Sheets and Hollins, 7–28.

Brown, Stephen. "Orphans of Oppression: The Passive Resistance of Bicultural Alienation." In Greenbaum, 53–69.

Cole, Michael. *Cultural Psychology: A Once and Future Discipline.* Cambridge, MA: Harvard University Press, 1996.

DeStigter, Todd. *Reflections of a Citizen Teacher: Literacy, Democracy, and the Forgotten Students of Addison High.* Urbana, IL: NCTE, 2001.

Dewey, John. *Democracy and Education: An Introduction to the Philosophy of Education.* New York: Macmillan, 1921.

Duffy, Helen. "Taking an Anthropological Stance: Implications for Supervising New Teachers." *English Education*, 33.2, 136–45, January 2001.

Ellsworth, Elizabeth. *Teaching Positions: Difference, Pedagogy and the Power of Address.* New York: Teachers College Press, 1997.

Fox, Tom. "Race and Collective Resistance." In Greenbaum, 71–86.

Gibson, Michelle, Martha Marinara, & Deborah Meem. "Bi, Butch, and Bar Dyke: Pedagogical Performances of Class, Gender, and Sexuality. *College Composition and Communication*, 52.1, 69–95, September 2000.

Giroux, Henry A. *Pedagogy and the Politics of Hope: Theory, Culture, and Schooling.* Boulder, CO: Westview Press, 1997.

Greenbaum, Andrea (Ed.). *Insurrections: Approaches to Resistance in Composition Studies.* New York: State University of New York, 2001.

Hardin, Joe Marshall. *Opening Spaces: Critical Pedagogy and Resistance Theory in Composition.* New York: State University of New York, 2001.

Hollins, Etta R. "Ethnic and Racial Identity and Teaching." In Sheets and Hollins, 183–93.

Johnson, Margaret J., & Kathryn Button. "Connecting Graduate Education in Language Arts with Teaching Contexts: The Power of Action Research." *English Education*, 32.2, 107–26, January 2000.

Marshall, Ian, & Wendy Ryden. "Interrogating the Monologue: Making Whiteness Visible." *College Composition and Communication*, 52.2, 240-59, December 2000.

Mead, George H. *Mind, Self, and Society: From the Standpoint of a Social Behaviorist.* Chicago: University of Chicago Press, 1934.

Pixley, Marcella Fleischman & Laura Schneider VanDerPloeg. "Learning to See: White." *English Education*, 32.4, 278–89, July 2000.

Rogoff, Barbara. *Apprenticeship in Thinking: Cognitive Development in Social Context.* New York: Oxford University Press, 1990.

Sheets, Rosa Hernandez. "Relating Competence in an Urban Classroom to Ethnic Identity Development." In Sheets and Hollins, 157–78.

Sheets, Rosa Hernandez, & Etta R. Hollins (Eds.). *Racial and Ethnic Identity in School Practices.* Mahwah, NJ: Lawrence Erlbaum, 1999.

Tussman, Joseph. *Experiment at Berkeley.* New York: Oxford University Press, 1969.

Vygotsky, Lev S. *Educational Psychology.* Boca Raton, FL: St. Lucie Press, 1997 (First published 1926, in Russian).

Weedon, Chris. *Feminism, Theory and the Politics of Difference.* London: Blackwell, 1999.

CHAPTER TWO
Equalizers: Allowing All Voices to Be Heard

"She muted her colors and blended in," writes R. A. Sasaki of the protagonist in her short story "The Loom" (1988). "She was a quiet student and the other children got used to her; some were even nice to her. But she was still not really a part of their world because she was not herself " (142). The only Japanese child in her class, the girl described here speaks little because she feels different and marginalized. Uncomfortable with a language that is not native to her and unfamiliar with hakujin (white American) customs, she keeps quiet in school, worried that her words never "conveyed what she really felt, what she really was, because what she really was unacceptable" (142). Many children share these kinds of feelings, often even those who belong to the dominant culture. Girls of any background can and do feel unacceptable in a culture that seems to have been created for boys.[1]

School experiences often appear to reinforce rather than weaken these perceptions. As a result, schoolgirls may become increasingly more timid as speakers and writers. In a very real sense, language fails them. This article highlights some causes for silence in schoolgirls and other marginalized students (members of minorities, students with learning disabilities, those who are physically challenged, etc.) and suggests ways teachers can help these students participate more fully as speakers and writers in language arts classes. It also shows how language arts instruction can change students' attitudes about themselves as gendered subjects, agents, and communicators.

Unfortunately, like the proverbial squeaky wheel that gets the oil, children who speak up in class—those who make either positive or negative noise—tend to receive more of the teacher's attention. Quiet children, and especially quiet girls, often get overlooked. To further complicate this issue, the nature of silence may not necessarily be restricted to lack of speech; it may also refer to speech that is not heard by others or not valued and which, therefore, has the same effect as no speech at all. Some youngsters chatter, hum, or speak during class but are generally disregarded; they also fit the category of silent students. As a longtime teacher of English, Spanish, and French in classes that range from grade six to adult classes, and as a current professor of English Education, I have come to believe that teachers who understand what silences children are better able to help them find their voices and, consequently, help them receive a more individualized education. Since the basis of language arts education is communication—reading, writing, speaking—it is essential that youngsters in these programs speak and write freely. They must also be listened and responded to in such a way that they believe what they say matters.

Proponents of democratic education have for decades encouraged equal education for all and have worked diligently to achieve its goals. This agenda has been reinvestigated in the 1980s and 1990s with feminist theorists (Lewis, 1993; Maher, 1987; McCracken & Appleby, 1992; Rubin, 1993; Schniedewind, 1985) leading the way toward a "gender pedagogy" (Maher, 1987) which moves beyond equality into the recognition and celebration of difference. Based on an extended application of Paulo Freire's (1970) "liberation" model, oppressed and silent groups find empowerment through "a different, more expressive, subjective, and participatory mode of learning than is validated by traditional models of education" (Maher, 1987, p. 92). Those considered oppressed include females, people of color, and any students who are culturally different, poor, or working class—a set of descriptors that covers the majority of students in many schools. Teachers who serve this student population can employ nontraditional methods to turn student silence into positive noise. In this chapter, I am particularly interested in the position of girls (elementary school age) and young women (middle school through high school) in the classroom. There is ample evidence to suggest that the reactions and behaviors associated with the marginalization of girls also hold true for other student groups, including students with disabilities, feminized males, and ethnic and racial minorities. Focusing on gender provides a starting point for moving toward more encompassing change involving other silenced groups.

Causes of Silence

It might seem that teachers could increase female student participation by making a greater effort to call on girls for answers, but, in fact, girls remain silent for complex reasons and often refuse to speak—or they may respond only in the most minimal way possible—even when directly called upon.

Examining the complex motivations for female silence can help teachers develop strategies to encourage change.

Girls Are Socialized to Be Polite

Feminists like Flynn (1998) recall efforts to make education gender blind and to train all students by the same methods. This denial of difference often resulted in continuation of already determined norms. Unfortunately, traditional norms favor males over females, white over color, rich over poor, and upper class over lower. If schools perpetuate this standard, many children suffer.

Studies show that in American classrooms, boys tend to get more attention than girls because they demand more (Coates, 1986; Orenstein, 1995; Sadker & Sadker, 1986). Males interrupt females frequently and dominate both large and small group discussions, whereas females usually respond in groups by offering supportive comments or they remain silent (Kramerae, 1981; Lakoff, 1975; Spender, 1980). Certainly there are assertive females, but, generally speaking, females are not held in high regard by other group members if they interrupt or demand attention. These behaviors are considered "unladylike" and, therefore, unacceptable. In addition, as indicated by a *New York Times* report (January 6, 1991), girls "emerge from adolescence with a poor self-image, relatively low expectations from life and much less confidence in themselves and their abilities than boys" (qtd. in McCracken, p. 60). These social behaviors and attitudes cannot be accounted for by looking at family influences; schools must bear some responsibility for discouraging girls' positive views of themselves as learners and achievers.

For instance, in their seminal investigation of female psychology, published in 1986, Belenky et al. report that men in our culture are more likely to do the speaking and women are more likely to listen. They suggest that these kinds of "sex differences are large and persistent and have been noted in private as well as in public domains" (Belenky et al., p. 45). These authors also suggest that boys enjoy and benefit from the competitive nature of American education but that cooperation is more amenable to girls' learning style.

This focus by females on cooperation and collaboration was highlighted for me in a recent discussion of teamwork that I observed. The discussion followed the play period in a mixed-gender physical education class for seventh and eighth graders. When asked to define teamwork, the girls said it meant "sticking together," not telling other people's secrets, helping people "instead of making them feel like fools," and following rules. The boys said it meant playing together, "not getting physical with teammates," and "not cussing at the referee." These comments suggest that girls were interested in building relationships through play, whereas boys seemed more concerned about making sure they did not get kicked off the team or benched. The females in this group also wanted to know if their team could have cheerleaders, suggesting that they would be as happy (or happier) to cheer the team on as they would be to play on the team. These girls saw teamwork as a chance to negotiate and improve relationships; the boys saw it as being necessary to allow the continued enjoyment of competitive activities.

Such patterns echo the findings of a 1997 survey in which Wherry reports that both winning and losing in academic competitions are unacceptable to bright adolescent females; therefore, most choose not to compete; competing to be "best" seems to set them apart, running counter to the "be nice" and "care for others" messages they've received (328). This socialized politeness places females in the role of hiding their abilities.

Girls Are Afraid to Break the Norms

All children want to be accepted. They need positive feedback from parents, from teachers, and—especially as they get older—from their peers. Unfortunately, girls receive mixed messages about what will make them acceptable, as indicated in Wherry's 1997 study of bright girls in grades seven, eight, and nine. The study's female participants believed their parents wanted them to do well in school but did not have the same expectations of them that they had of their brothers. In these girls' views, boys were expected to succeed outside of the family. Girls, on the other hand, were expected to become nurturers who might have to support themselves with their careers but whose major concern should be building relationships. To achieve these mixed goals, girls in Wherry's (1997) study felt that although boys are "rude, loud, and physically active" (327), girls should be polite and modest. Girls were willing to share their perceived weaknesses with others, but not their strengths. They felt that "although they were at the top of their class, it was best to achieve in silence" (328).

This silence may result from teachers not waiting long enough for them to think about the question and formulate an answer (Townsend & Fu, 1998). Short leader wait times may hinder boys, but most boys remain willing to take risks, guess, call out answers, and raise hands even if they do not know the answers. By contrast, girls become increasingly more silent. The disturbing paradox here is that students who remain quiet learn less, yet teachers reward girls more for silence than for risk-taking. Orenstein's (1995) observations of teachers and student interaction indicate that "the lessons of the hidden curriculum teach girls to value silence and compliance, to view those qualities as a virtue" (35). One girl says "teachers like us because we're nicer, quieter, and better behaved" (Orenstein, 1995, p. 35). In other words, the system encourages girls to venture less even though the outcome may be that they learn less.

Further evidence that females are taught to follow rules and tend to do so much more regularly than males can be found in a recent survey (Great Divide, 1996). The results of that survey indicated that 99% of girls and 73% of boys felt girls behave more responsibly than boys. Observations of seventh and eighth graders in a private school setting are illustrative. In a mixed-gender physical education class, girls followed directions and tried to perform the proper movements for each teacher-directed exercise. The boys in the class fooled around, kicked the wall, and generally disregarded instructions until the teacher initiated a competitive situation to determine which students could perform the most sit-ups. At this point, the boys got interested and tried to outdo one another but without regard to proper sit-up form. This contrasted sharply with the girls, who continued to concentrate on form even in the heat of competition. Clearly, doing what they had been told mattered more to the females than winning the competition.

Normative influences on girls are not restricted to day-to-day interactions but also on future expectation. Girls continue to have different expectations in terms of home life and careers. In a 1996 (Great Divide) survey of more than 200,000 American teenagers, 81% of the girls surveyed and 82% of the boys felt that boys generally have more career opportunities than girls. For example, only 58% of the girls and 52% of the boys felt that a woman would be elected President of the United States in their lifetime.

According to Wherry's (1997) study, girls have few positive role models for achievement. Instead they get the message that they have to look good. Girls do not support each others' intellectual pursuits but often reward good looks and popularity. My observations of a seventh-grade mathematics class provide illustration. In this case, when the students were allowed to converse, boys commented on the difficulty of math, on their preference for science, and on their frustrations in working problems. The female students discussed their relationships with males: "She thinks I like Tom, but I don't" and "If I had to choose between Dave, Tom or Bill, I'd choose...."

Such patterns suggest that not only are females concerned about following the rules, but they also tend to concentrate on relationships with males. Orenstein (1995) found similar responses. She quotes one eighth-grade female student who says, "School isn't as important as your friends...and you can't have a good social life and good grades. That's just the way it is" (106). In instance after instance, girls show that they buy into a normative double standard. They acquiesce to the belief that males are supposed to dominate in the school environment, even if it means breaking rules, yet girls are supposed to concentrate on relationships and remain silent or unheard when it comes to academic activity.

Girls Lack Self-Esteem

Perhaps as a consequence of this double standard, some girls begin to feel that they cannot achieve much in school—certainly not as much as males can achieve. Orenstein says, "Our culture devalues both women and the qualities which it projects onto us, such as nurturance, cooperation, and intuition. It has taught us to undervalue ourselves" (xix). Because those things women do well tend to elicit few rewards, women come to feel that what they do is not important. In academics, this can provoke a loss of confidence, and "the confidence drop often precedes the competence drop: even in early adolescence, girls who perform as well as boys often evaluate their skills as lesser " (Orenstein, 1995, p. 18). Thus a downward spiral becomes established in which women become progressively less successful academically as they move toward high school graduation.

Girls Are Angry

Educators make a serious mistake if they believe that female silence means acquiescence. Orenstein (1995) shows how when girls repeatedly are ignored by teachers in favor of more vocal and insistent boys, they shut up, stop trying, and become sullen. One young woman puts her head down on her desk and says she hates the class. Orenstein observes in this student and others "a kind of passive resistance to participation by the girls that went unquestioned by the teacher" (24).

I observed a similar dynamic in a college freshman English class where the young teaching assistant called mostly on white males, whether they volunteered or not, to answer questions about the reading assignment. This teacher always wrote a summary of their answers on the chalkboard. He called on black men, too, although less often, and also wrote down their comments. White women did not volunteer, but the teacher did call on a few. Not only did he fail to write their comments on the board, but he sometimes also made little jokes about the inadequacy of their answers. This teacher did not call on either of the two black women in class; these women remained silent. When I mentioned this pattern to the teacher after class, he was astonished. His behavior had been totally unconscious, and he had not noticed the low rate of female participation.

In situations like this, women and girls keep quiet in silent protest of what they recognize, at least subconsciously, to be an unfair situation. The anger may not surface because of their ingrained politeness, but it smolders beneath the surface. Occasionally, it will burst forth in the direction of the teacher, but more often the anger is directed inward. Girls seem to expect to be treated this way, yet they resent it. In his discussion of identity negotiation, Brooke (1991) talks about "the importance of resistance, the need of people on the margins to refuse to assent to definitions of self and reality which dominant institutions seek to impose on them" (122). Rather than verbalizing their resistance, because aggressive language is not considered appropriate behavior for young females, schoolgirls often express their anger by silence and a stubborn refusal to participate, or more subtly and ultimately more damaging to them, by a minimal kind of participation resulting in passing grades but little real learning. This pattern may be so familiar and so easily confused with girls knowing the answers but pretending they do not, that teachers fail to recognize it as rebellion.

How Language and Literacy Can Help Female Students

Gender-related silence is a problem that has been centuries in the making. Surely, there is no quick fix that will change the way classrooms are set up or the way males and females relate to one another. Orenstein (1995) says "to effect true change, we must alter the way we raise our boys as well as our girls" (xxi), and this is the work of decades, not days. There are, however, many ways language and literacy can be used to improve the situation and to help women find their classroom voices.

Discuss Socialization

Maher (1997) warns against trying to become gender blind and suggests instead that we openly challenge the status quo. Teachers have generally resisted open discussion of gender, and, indeed, it would be reasonable to assume that such discussion would be dominated by men in the classroom just as men dominate most discussions there. This means that other methods must be devised which allow for an exchange of ideas and discovery of new possibilities but which do not pit males against females. Most importantly, all students must be encouraged to take part. Townsend and Fu (1998) recommend small group or paired talk as a means to achieve this, and certainly talking is easier in small groups than in large ones. I would also recommend the use of same-sex groups or pairs. This eliminates any possibility of male dominance, gives females greater opportunity for self-expression, removes the dynamics involved in male-female sexual interplay, and impels at least some women to speak in their groups. In fact, women welcome same-gender groupings to the point where many females who are serious about their education choose all-female courses (Wilson, 1995). In a 1996 (Great Divide) survey, 41% of girls who responded said they would take a same-sex class if it were offered. In my own classes, postgroup processing sessions (discussions led by the teacher that focus on the way the grouped worked, what was accomplished, and what problems arose) show that women enjoy being in groups without men at least part of the time.

Group discussions can and should sometimes center on gender issues but should also be used to work on ordinary class assignments. After a series of group discussions alternating same-gender and mixed-gender combinations, full-class processing might address such questions as "Which kind of group did you like better and why?" and "Who was the leader in your same-gender group? Was it the same people who led mixed-gender groups?" Another possible question might be "What issues would you feel more comfortable discussing only with people of your gender?" This processing focuses on gender without moralizing and helps students look objectively at group dynamics.

Teachers should also intervene in classroom situations where one gender, or one individual, tries to control discussion and silence opposition. For some reason, perhaps because many teachers are women and have been socialized themselves to be polite, teachers often hesitate to break into group discussions or to ask domineering students to be quiet. In fact, this practice can be beneficial to all students, especially the quiet ones. A teacher can speak privately with a particularly outspoken student and ask that person to remain silent for a class period, but there is nothing wrong with interrupting a habitual interrupter and saying, for instance, "Henry, please let other students have a chance to speak" or "Jerome, we have heard the male point of view; now I would prefer to hear what a woman has to say about this issue."

Foster Norm-breaking, Risk-taking

One way language arts teachers can encourage muted students to think and talk about their timidity as speakers and writers is to assign readings about girls/women (and boys/men) who do not follow the norm. Biographies of famous women like Eleanor Roosevelt or relative unknowns like the female pilots of the early twentieth century can lead to discussion about positive kinds of risk-taking and rule-breaking. Fiction can also be provocative. Young students, for example, can read Betty Greene's (1973) novel *Summer of My German Soldier* and then talk about parents' expectations concerning their daughters and about the morality of breaking rules to help another human being. This is only one example from many possible choices of readings that might lead to fruitful discussion and example. As Spiegel (1998) points out, "besides relating characters' feelings and experiences to their own lives, students also have been found to use literature to help them make personal choices" (44). Some of these choices may involve girls and women asserting themselves and acknowledging their own abilities.

In all discussions, teachers can help quiet students (as well as vocal ones) by allowing more time for them to think about and compose responses to questions. Levin and Nolan (1996) estimate that teachers wait an average of only 2.6 seconds between question and answer. If no one blurts out an answer, teachers either supply the answer or call on an individual (often one they know is likely to answer correctly, and often a male) to supply it. This practice favors males who feel freer to take the risk of answering incorrectly and squelches females who, according to Belenky et al. (1986), prefer to think carefully before answering.

In addition to waiting longer for considered answers (a minute or two seems like forever to teachers who are used to waiting only seconds), teachers can employ other strategies to help all students become involved in discussion. They can, for instance, give lists of questions along with reading assignments and instruct students to research, talk to their parents and friends, think about possible answers, and take notes. Thus armed for discussion, quiet students are more likely to participate. Another technique requires students to compose their own questions about assigned material. They can test their questions in small groups and then throw them into a grab bag. When the teacher selects questions to ask the entire class, chances are good that each student will know the answers to at least those questions which came from her group and that all students will feel more able to contribute without fear of embarrassment.

Freewriting also warms up students for discussions. Teachers can present a question and then allow ten minutes or so for students to write their thoughts on paper, perhaps suggesting that they share their writing with a partner if they choose to do so. Then every student will have thought about the question and may feel more prepared to speak. Students can be encouraged to take further risks in writing through the use of ungraded activities or deferred grading. When the fear of being graded is removed or postponed, girls and other hesitant writers feel freer to say what they feel. Deferred grading through the use of end-of-semester portfolios allows students to select which papers will be submitted to the teacher. Knowing they will be able to withhold some of their writing and keep it private enables writers to express themselves without restraint.

Use Cooperative Pedagogy to Teach Reading and Writing

Belenky et al. (1986) determined that females have trouble in school because traditional methodology does not suit their favored learning style. For example, many girls are less comfortable with competition than boys, yet competition is basic to traditional public school pedagogy. Females do better in collaborative, cooperative environments supervised by nurturing teachers who encourage rather than criticize and who allow every student opportunities to contribute and receive praise (Belenky et al., 1986; Johnson & Johnson, 1974; Slavin et al., 1985). This means that teachers can empower girls and young women as speakers and writers by planning activities where they work closely with others, sharing ideas and responsibilities, presenting findings together, even sometimes receiving the same grade for a community project. In the past, this kind of behavior may have been viewed as cheating, but, in fact, students may learn more from an exchange of ideas than from other methods. Horning (1987) claims that "for many of us, real learning does not take place until we have to teach what we have learned to someone else" (68). Cooperative group work offers opportunities for shy students to serve as teachers, thus bolstering both learning and self-esteem.

Collaboration has to be properly monitored to be effective, especially when dealing with quiet students. In addition to grouping students carefully, teachers should assign each student a specific group role (recorder, presenter, timekeeper, encourager, etc.) to ensure participation; role assignments should be random, not self-selected, because shy youngsters will seldom volunteer for the role of presenter, for example, if allowed to be the silent recorder instead. Teachers should move about the classroom during collaborative work sessions and intervene where necessary to make sure everyone takes part so that no single member (or group of members) dominates activities to the exclusion of others.

Allow Expression of Anger

Even in language arts classes that are based on communication, some students refuse to participate in discussions, collaboration, or other activities because they are angry. Girls may feel no one hears them, so they refuse to speak or write. They may try to punish a teacher who never calls on them or who favors other, louder students. Certain techniques can help overcome this type of resistance and make formerly silent students more willing to join class activities.

One such technique is writing in a journal. Cinthia Gannett (1992) suggests that women respond particularly well to journal writing. The personal narrative seems more amenable to their writing style than researched academic papers, and many women find daily writing helps them organize and reflect on their lives and on what they are learning in school. If journals are not collected by teachers or read by others, they may serve as a place to express frustrations and to release anger. When teachers do collect journals, they may, through careful reading, discover what bothers silent students about the class and their place in it. These readings can provide opportunities for one-on-one conferencing.

Conferencing can also be effective without the use of journals. Although time-consuming, regular meetings between teacher and student can make a big difference in the life of a quiet class member and can gradually change the student's attitude toward the teacher, the other students, and even the subject matter.

Letter or memo writing may serve as an addendum to or, when necessary due to time constraints, take the place of face-to-face conferences. When students have e-mail capability, they may enjoy exchanging memos with other students and with the teacher. This informal communication has the advantage of being distant yet providing a fairly rapid response, certainly faster than waiting for a teacher to grade a set of papers and return them. If e-mail is not available, or as an adjunct to the memo, students can be encouraged (or required) to exchange letters with the teacher or someone else. Besides offering writing practice, letters may serve as a good place for students who feel marginalized to express their concerns and complaints privately without fear of repercussions.

Language arts teachers have many opportunities to organize class debates and to assign argumentative writing, both of which can help diffuse anger. Debates about gender, power dynamics, prejudice, and other controversial topics encourage students to look at both sides of a given issue. The formal debate process demonstrates that it is all right to have divergent opinions and that arguing can be sanctioned rather than criticized as impolite. "Losing" can also be deconstructed when one is required to argue a position with which one does not necessarily agree.

Argumentative writing can be used as a processing technique after any kind of group activity. Students might, for example, be asked to argue for or against same-gender groups. This gives quiet girls an opportunity to complain about boys who dominate group work. Or the teacher might ask for an argument in favor of the individual's right to be heard. Here the boys also have the opportunity to protest the teacher's intervention; some of my students use this venue to complain about my equity agenda. This often leads to a discussion about whether it is fair to silence the vocal group to allow the quiet students to be heard. I am always gratified when formerly quiet students shout their opinions during this kind of discussion because it indicates that change is beginning to take place. Even if no discussion ensues, students feel better when they have an opportunity to express their personal opinions in writing.

Another way of allowing students to vent their anger is to have them grade other group members in the course of a collaborative activity. In a group of four, for example, students can be asked to submit to the teacher, without showing their response to other students, their opinion of what percentage of the work each group member did. Given a 100% total, the ideal split for a group of four would be 25% each. However, an individual may feel she or he has done 50% of the work and another member 0%. When the teacher takes such student input seriously and assigns participation grades accordingly, nonvocal students who do indeed work hard gain a sense of empowerment and learn that anger can bring justice. The danger of one person's momentary pique negatively influencing another's grade is mitigated by the fact that the opinion of all group members is considered. In addition to providing an outlet to frustration, this method is quite effective in identifying loafers or freeloaders and giving credit to quiet hard workers.

All of these techniques may help relieve tensions felt by angry students. As anger abates, formerly silent students may feel more willing to join the classroom conversation.

Conclusion

At the close of a long school day, teachers may wish for silence. In terms of providing the best education for every student, however, they are well served to encourage productive noise while class is in session. In language arts classes, this noise should include the voices of all students, not least among them girls and young women who, under other circumstances, might remain silent or unheard.

In my own classes and others I have observed, I have found that focusing on gender can promote positive change. I believe we must stop assuming that presenting material in the same way to all students makes language arts education equitable. Instead, we should recognize the value of difference and select materials and methods appropriate to different students. A Mexican American girl will not necessarily enjoy the same books as a white boy, nor will she respond to the same writing topics. An adolescent woman is unlikely to participate in discussions dominated by a group of teenage men unless she is backed by a strong female chorus.

The language arts classroom offers an ideal venue for instituting change. Teachers can create an atmosphere that encourages all students to read, discuss, and write—an atmosphere where the goal is not to blend in, but to stand out and speak up.

NOTE

This article originally appeared in *Language Arts* 77.4 (March 2000) under the title "Muted Colors: Gender and Classroom Silence," author Elaine Fredericksen. Copyright 2000 by the National Council of Teachers of English: Reprinted with permission.

WORKS CITED

American Association of University Women. *Gender and Race on the Campus and in the School: Beyond Affirmative Action.* Symposium proceedings presented at the 1997 AAUW college/university symposium, Anaheim, CA, June 1997.

Belenky, Mary F., B. Clinchy, N. Goldberger, & J. Tarule. *Women's Ways of Knowing: The Development of Self, Voice, and Mind.* New York: Basic Books, 1986.

Brooke, R. E. *Writing and Sense of Self: Identity Negotiation in Writing Workshops.* Urbana, IL: National Council of Teachers of English, 1991.

Coates, J. W*omen, Men, and Language.* London & New York: Longman, 1986.

Flynn, Elizabeth. "Composing as a Woman." *College Composition and Communication,* 39 (4), 423–35, 1988.

Freire, Paulo. *Pedagogy of the Oppressed.* New York: Herder and Herder, 1970.

———. *The Politics of Education: Culture, Power and Liberation.* South Hadley, MA: Bergin & Garvey, 1985.

Gannett, Cinthia. *Gender and the Journal: Diaries and Academic Discourse.* Albany, NY: State University of New York Press, 1992.

"Great Divide: Teens and the Gender Gap." *El Paso Times,* 6 September, 1996: A–26.

Greene, Bette. *Summer of My German Soldier.* New York: Doubleday, 1973.

Horning, Alice S. "The 'Climate of Fear' in the Teaching of Writing." In C. L. Caywood & G. R. Overing (Eds.), *Teaching Writing: Pedagogy, Gender, and Equity* (pp. 51–84). Albany, NY: State University of New York Press, 1987.

Johnson David W., & R. T. Johnson. Instructional Goal Structure: Cooperative Competitive or Individualistic. *Review of Education Research,* 44 (2), 213–40, 1974.

Kramerae, Cheris. *Women and Men Speaking: Framework for Analysis.* Rowley, MA: Newbury, 1981.

Lakoff, Robin. *Language and Woman's Place.* New York: Harper, 1975.

Levin, James & J. F. Nolan. *Principles of Classroom Management* (2nd ed.) Needham Heights, MA: Allyn & Bacon, 1996.

Lewis, Magda. G. *Without a Word: Teaching Beyond Women's Silence.* New York: Routledge, 1993.

Maher, Frances. "Toward a Richer Theory of Feminist Pedagogy: A Comparison of the 'Liberation' and 'Gender' Models for Teaching and Learning." *Journal of Education,* 169 (3), 91–100, 1987.

Maher, Frances. "Progressive Education and Feminist Pedagogy: Issues in Gender, Power and Authority." In (no Eds.), *Gender and Race on the Campus and in the School: Beyond Affirmative Action* (pp. 237–50). Annapolis Junction, MD: American Association of University Women, 1997.

McCracken, Nancy. "Regendering the Reading of Literature." In N. McCracken & B. Appleby (Eds.), *Gender Issues in the Teaching of English (* 55–68). Portsmouth, NH: Boynton/Cook, 1992.

Orenstein, Peggy. *School Girls: Young Women, Self-esteem, and the Confidence Gap.* New York: Doubleday, 1995.

Rubin, Donalee. *Gender Influences: Reading Student Texts.* Carbondale, IL: Southern Illinois Press, 1993.

Sadker, Myra P. & D. M. Sadker. Sexism in the Classroom: From Grade School to Graduate School. *Phi Delta Kappan,* 67 (7), 512–15, 1986.

Sasaki, R. A. "The Loom." In P. A. Richard-Amato (Ed.), *World Views: Multicultural Literature for Critical Writers, Reader, and Thinkers* (pp. 137–57). Belmont, CA: Wadsworth Publishing, 1989.

Schniedewind, N. Cooperatively structured learning: Implications for feminist pedagogy. *Journal of Thought,* 20 (3), 74–87, 1985.

Slavin, R., S. Sharan, S. Kagan, R. Hertz Lazarowitz, C. Web, & R. Schmuck. *Learning to Cooperate, Cooperating to Learn.* New York: Plenum, 1985.

Spender, D. *Man Made Language.* London: Routledge, 1980.

Spiegel, D. L. Reader Response Approaches and the Growth of Readers. *Language Arts,* 76 (1), 41–48, 1998.

Townsend, J. S. & D. Fu. Quiet Students across Cultures and Contexts. *English Education,* 31 (1), 4–19, 1998.

Wherry, S. "No Wonder I Don't Know Who I Am!": Messages from peers, parents, and the media as perceived by bright adolescent females. In (no Eds.), *Gender and Race on the Campus and in the School: Beyond Affirmative Action* (325–30). Annapolis Junction, MD: American Association of University Women, 1997.

Wilson, R. For Women Only? *Chronicle of Higher Education*, July 18, 1995: A17.

CHAPTER THREE
Collaborators: Creating Writing Communities for a Diverse Student Population

> "I didn't think I could do college-level writing."
> "I was afraid everyone else would write better."
> "I remember coming into English class the first day. I was scared to death."

These comments from my students are typical of first-year college entrants, but they take on added significance because I teach on the border between Mexico and the United States. Our campus is third in the nation for the number of Hispanic students it graduates. Sixty-six percent of our student body is Hispanic (mainly Mexican American), and a large percentage of students in most of my classes come from families where Spanish is the first language. My students are people of color, people of a unique culture, and I believe this makes a difference in how they learn and how they write. Furthermore, as a white female teacher, I represent the "other" in my classes. If I am to teach effectively, I must find ways to address issues of difference and make them work for rather than against us. Without essentializing my students or myself, I must negotiate difference in positive ways.

Catherine Prendergast (1998) calls race "the absent presence in composition studies" (36) and worries that "without significant changes to the profession and pedagogy, women and people of color will continue to wind up on the bottom" (50) in terms of educational opportunity. She urges composition theorizations "that do not reinscribe people of color as either foreign or invisible" (51). My purpose in this chapter is to focus on Mexican Americans in first-year writing courses and to argue for a community approach as a way to satisfy their special pedagogical needs. Although this study refers specifically to college freshmen, I believe its implications extend to Hispanic students in other writing situations, including those in secondary schools.

Learning community pedagogy has a long history, and readers who know that history may assume that this is old hat, that such methods are already widely used. They are not. In spite of years of study, learning communities represent radical pedagogy. Most secondary schools, colleges, and universities still take a traditional approach to education, and few make special allowances for differences in minority learning style preferences. This may account for the poor success rate of minority students, and most particularly Hispanics, in higher education.

Problems and Implications

The U.S. Census Bureau reports that "as of 1997, the U.S. population included 29.7 million Hispanics," about 35% of whom were under age 18 (Hispanic Population). The National Council of La Raza estimates that within the next ten years Hispanics will be the largest minority group in the United States, outnumbering the presently larger population of African Americans (Study Says). These statistics suggest tremendous need for programs to effectively educate ever-growing numbers of Hispanic Americans, but we seem to be failing at this important task.

Records of poor performance and frequent school dropouts indicate that Hispanics do have special needs. A 1998 report by the National Council of La Raza notes "the nation's burgeoning Latino population is lagging far behind other racial and ethnic groups in educational achievement from pre-kindergarten through college" (Study Says). This La Raza study shows only seven of ten Hispanic students stay in secondary school, and only 34% of Hispanic high school graduates go on to college. In spite of my own university's success in graduating minority students, we still have alarmingly poor rates of retention with 35% dropping out in the freshman year and 72% overall attrition.

Our students want to stay in school until graduation, but they face many obstacles, particularly in classes that include a writing component. All college students are at risk of poor performance in such classes if they come from lower-class families, if they perceive themselves or are perceived by others as "different" or "marginal," if they are first-generation college students, and if English is not their native language or where so-called non-standard English is, in fact, standard for use in their own homes and neighborhoods. This pattern describes many Hispanic students currently enrolled in U.S. schools. Because their communication styles differ from the classroom norm or from the norm the teacher considers appropriate, these students may be labeled illiterate or barely literate, placing them in "that condition of 'economic disadvantage' associated with the most oppressed people in our society" (Holzman, 299). Educators need methods to dispel such labels and to ensure Hispanics equal opportunities for success. My experience suggests that learning communities can help in these endeavors.

Hispanic students learn quickly that school language, especially written language, may differ considerably from that which they speak and write at home, and they soon realize that their home language may provide obstacles at school. Perceptions of difference continue through college enrollment. One report says Mexican American college students "felt that they were not properly prepared in areas such as reading, writing, and studying which are the more cognitive and academic proficiencies of the language" (Garcia-Vazquez et al., 7). Their feelings are substantiated by achievement test scores that indicate "only a small percentage of Mexican Americans appear to have the requisite basic skills to persevere in higher education" (Carter, Segura, 71), and Suarez et al. suggest that a "combination of acculturational and developmental stress may be particularly difficult for Hispanic college students" (491). Many first-year college students approach writing tasks with varying degrees of shame and trepidation that hinder their ability to write freely and successfully. The studies mentioned here indicate that Mexican American students, especially those from low socioeconomic situations, may have reasonable bases for their worries. Radical pedagogy is required to improve the minority education situation.

Benefits of Cooperative Learning

Teachers can empower nontraditional students by assigning material that is meaningful to them and by forming and nurturing classroom learning communities. Cooperative activities, collaborative learning, and non-competitive game playing in the writing classroom appear particularly amenable to the learning style of Mexican Americans. Studies like those of Spencer Kagan (1985) suggest that "Mexican American children display a more cooperative orientation than their Anglo American peers" (In Slavin et al., 258) and can be expected to perform better in cooperative rather than competitive situations. This suggestion is supported by Suarez et al., who believe "emphasis on individual effort and competition may not be as effective in teaching Hispanic students as encouraging cooperation and group efforts" (502). Of course, not all members of any group fit generalized categories, and plenty of Mexican Americans thrive on competition. Still, if cooperation offers promise to large numbers of students, it seems reasonable for educators to offer it at least as an option to common competitive methodology. My own students, used to school competition, sometimes resist the learning community format at first, especially when it involves sharing grades with other group members, but they almost all end the semester feeling good about their groups, about their progress, and about themselves.

Not only does cooperation appear to help ethnic minority and other non-traditional students, but studies also indicate that competitive school activities actually harm these young learners. Kagan and his colleagues claim in "Classroom Structural Bias" (1985) "considerable theoretical support" indicating that traditional competitive U.S. public school systems "discriminate against the achievement, the cultural values, and the well-being of Mexican American and black students" (in Slavin et al., 277). Learning communities mitigate against such discrimination. Rather than belittling the culture of nontraditional students, cooperative educational practices encourage shared experience, thus reducing feelings of otherness that might hinder learning.

Learning communities where students work together in cohesive groups to solve problems or prepare projects can heighten their sense of belonging, lessen their apprehension, and offer them multiple opportunities to develop facility with a wide variety of writing and thinking assignments. Because base groups (semester-long study teams) are essentially self-governed, members do not feel dominated by instructors who may represent a different culture and pressure to assimilate. When students study together outside of class, they may speak their home language or dialect. Many of my students do their research in Spanish-language texts that they then discuss with their teammates. Also, if they disagree with something from a textbook or a lecture, they can talk about it among friends. If they wish to, they can approach the instructor together and present their divergent view, secure that they will have the support of others who understand their position. This process fosters pride and self-confidence by making students feel successful and supported. It encourages open discussion and assures students that they can learn without giving up basic beliefs. John Ogbu says "schools can and should establish programs to promote more trusting relations between them and minority students and communities" (85). Community approaches foster trust because they encourage students and teacher to communicate freely and to work together toward a common goal.

Learning communities can reduce the negative effects of stereotype threats in several ways. Claude M. Steele defines the phenomenon of stereotype threat as "the event of a negative stereotype about a group to which one belongs becoming self-relevant" (616). Mexican American students feeling normal first-year college jitters about a writing task may then assume, that their anxiety arises from the fact that Hispanics "can't write in English." That is, they apply negative stereotypes to themselves, even when there is no basis in truth. Steele cites a number of studies (Allport, 1954; Bettelheim, 1943; Clark, 1965; Grier & Coobs, 1968) indicating that minority group members internalize stereotypes and "the resulting sense of inadequacy becomes part of their personality" (617). The social environment of the university may encourage stereotype threat by promoting traditional ideologies that favor the white majority. Sylvia Hurtado suggests that minority students may be "generally undervalued (regardless of their achievement characteristics), whereas high achieving white students are viewed as resources" (544).

Perhaps the best way to remove inappropriate stereotype anxiety is to give students multiple experiences of success. Working in teams with minority and nonminority members can serve this purpose. Team projects take pressure off the individual, and successful completion of projects shows each member that s/he can function in the college writing environment. High team grades, community sharing of projects, congratulatory base-group sessions, and classroom celebrations can go a long way toward eliminating negative stereotypes.

How Learning Communities Work

A large body of scholarship exists on learning communities and how they function and can be easily accessed in any library database using the key words "learning communities" or "collaborative learning." What I offer here is a brief overview of implementation at one university and a summary of results with its mainly Mexican American student population.

Cooperative learning encompasses group work but goes beyond it to create cohesive classroom communities that, in the ideal form, include every student, as well as the teacher who serves as guide rather than judge. Clustering young people into permanent groups (called base groups) establishes the basis for the learning community. Sometimes they form other groups but return to the base group regularly for assigned tasks that ensure continued connection among members. Collaborative learning techniques allow students to make choices about what they read, what they write, and how they attack specific problems. This helps them overcome their initial aversion to writing and increases their confidence in their ability to express themselves. At the same time, feeling like a contributor to a communal effort eases worries about being different or not fitting in.

With this in mind, I place students in self-selected or randomly assigned base groups composed of four or five students who meet together throughout the semester or year. Base groups generally get together at the beginning of class to discuss a particular question (an issue that will arise in the reading for the day, perhaps, or an issue of local interest: "Why should the U.S. government support illegal immigrants?" or "Does NAFTA help or hurt border communities?"). Discussions often require as little as five minutes but act as a stimulus for later class discussion or individual writing. Groups might re-form at the end of the class to talk about changed attitudes, to approach consensus, to argue further, or to draw conclusions, but this is not always necessary. Base groups do usually get together for a few minutes at the end of each week to celebrate in some way. They might, for instance, talk about each member's greatest success for the week or simply wish one another a good weekend. The important element is continued contact over the long term.

Membership in long-term groups has positive effects on first-year college students who otherwise might join the dropout ranks. All participants share phone numbers and e-mail addresses with other group members. If any student misses more than one class, members of the group contact the missing person to find out the reason. They deliver homework assignments to anyone who is ill and, more importantly, urge a discouraged student to return with offers of assistance and assurance that no group member will be allowed to fail. This kind of group aid may particularly benefit minorities because "many ethnic minorities are first-generation college students and may not have the support or understanding of their families" (Rendon, 1994). In my community, it is not unheard of for parents to dissuade their children from attending college, preferring that they get jobs and contribute to family in more immediate ways. Among high school students, peer pressure from friends who have dropped out may tempt students away from their studies. In these situations, students need motivation from those school friends who realize the value of more distant goals.

Learning communities also provide strength in numbers. Where one student in trouble might hesitate to approach a busy teacher, entire groups seek out help en masse until they are sure their worried friend is back on track. Base groups very frequently become out-of-class study groups that buoy all participants and create strong bonds of collaboration and friendship. Our program began in 1995, and some original base groups from that year continued to sign up for classes and study together. They also graduated together. This pattern has repeated itself in more recent groups.

In addition to base groups, short-term groups serve many purposes. To practice writing arguments, for example, I often have students select a partner who is not in the same base group and ask them to choose a controversial issue from a list. The list may be generated from classroom brainstorming activities, taken from students' reading assignments, or focus on news of the day. A list in one of my recent classes included whether or not to ban smoking in local restaurants and bars, whether parents should be legally responsible for their children's wrongdoing, how to deal with a recent influx of street people, and whether children of illegal immigrants should receive free education in U.S. schools. These topics came from readings in the text that students had previously selected. Each team decided on a topic and worked together to create a list of pros and cons regarding that issue. When the partners had a substantial number of ideas, I asked them to get together with another pair of students working on the same topic so they could compare notes and expand their lists. The foursome then went to the library together as a research team to find support for both sides of the issue. Once the research was gathered, one member of each pair elected either the pro or con side and wrote a draft of an argument essay. The next day, they shared the draft with the other member of the foursome who was writing the same side of the argument. This provided a forum for discussing and expanding ideas. Each person then wrote a second draft to share with the entire foursome. At this point, each essay was examined for refutation—the inclusion and rebuttal of the best opposition arguments. Obviously discussing points of contention with opposition writers can provide useful insights. Each essay was then revised for a grade. Not only does this kind of multilevel assignment foster the process of writing and revision, but it also encourages interchange of ideas among students and facilitates bonding.

Teams provide support for students who feel underprepared and also help hone the skills of advanced learners. Rather than assigning individual writing tasks to students unsure of their abilities, students in learning communities form teams and tackle assignments together. Team members who most clearly understand the material explain it to others. One member may serve as the group grammarian and explain proofreading corrections, while another takes charge of organization or offers suggestions for creative additions to the group composition. This approach reduces fear of failure and makes writing a pleasant task rather than an ordeal. Alice Horning (1987) writes, "For many of us, real learning does not take place until we have to teach what we have learned to someone else" (68), and this is exactly what happens in collaborative classrooms where members of the learning community share what they know with other group members so the team can be successful. This means that a student who ordinarily may feel uncomfortable writing because of poor facility with English vocabulary can contribute in other ways, perhaps by doing valuable research or improving the logic of an argument. Each team member writes a portion of a report, but all sections are then scrutinized by other members who suggest revision and explain why change is necessary. Often they do this much more effectively than a teacher might, and students revise more willingly when they understand that communication is their goal rather than a grade. Final reports created by teamwork tend to show few of the errors typical in beginning writers because these have been discovered and handled in the team process.

Group assignments can successfully revolve around a real-life problem. One particularly productive exercise in my own class involved revising a poorly written information sheet about a solar-heating system for homes. Working in teams, the students analyzed the information and an accompanying diagram and decided what was wrong with the written information. They decided what needed to be included, added, or eliminated and also designed more accurate diagrams and/or illustrations. Then they created a new format for the information that served a promotional as well as an informational function. As the students collaborated, they taped their conversations, some of which took place during class and some outside. Their finished project included the brochure or information sheet. It also included a report on their collaboration which analyzed who in the group took leadership roles, who offered the most new ideas, who did most of the writing for the brochure, who designed the illustrations, who was the computer expert, who wrote the collaboration report (this had to be a different writer or writers from the brochure), and who did the most useful editing. The final products were exceptionally good; students expressed satisfaction with their work; and there was almost no second-language interference or low-level writing. The students understood that their purpose was to improve the original that was written in high-level language but was not clear. They managed, for the most part, to maintain the original level of linguistic sophistication while improving clarity and did this with no prompting from the teacher. Instead, as part of their group work, they prompted one another. This exercise was considerably more effective than some of the individual ones I assigned in the course because students attacked it with greater interest and less apprehension about their writing skills.

Once feelings of community develop, some projects can focus on cultural difference, thus foregrounding issues that matter to Hispanic students and their classmates. My students do not divide along ethnic lines when they discuss immigration law, for example. Rather divisions seem to be based on political inclinations and sometimes on economic background. Students used to working together toward consensus, as they must do to complete a group project, also develop skills in disagreeing amicably. A final report can as easily present various points of view as a single one; this kind of report gives students practice with innovative formatting and organization.

If students enter college feeling underprepared (feelings reportedly common and intense among Hispanics), they worry more about grades than do those students who consider themselves well prepared. This interferes with academic comfort. Saundra Tomlinson-Clarke sees comfort as an indicator of persistence in academic settings. To ease grade tension, I often use ungraded collaborative activities as an outcome of learning communities. In collaborative settings, working together toward a presentation can reward students so they do not require grades. When grading seems necessary, "non-traditional students particularly need to know that they will not be attacked or negatively criticized for what they write" (Fredericksen, 119–20). Deferring grades until after revision can help, as can group grades or

some form of collaborative grading. My students, for example, evaluate themselves and other members, thus having a say in their own grades. One kind of evaluation form has students anonymously rate the amount of work each group member has done by percentages: Student A might give herself credit for 40% of the work and credit Student B with another 40%. She might give Student C no credit at all and attribute the other 20% to Student D. When all evaluations are tallied, the teacher has a good idea of how to grade each team member's contribution. This practice relieves one problem with group activities—the tendency for an occasional student to let others do the majority of the work, while at the same time giving students a degree of autonomy that encourages self-esteem.

Many classes are very large, and procedures may be lecture-based, thus making formal learning communities difficult to manage. However, any class of any size can include collaboration as an aid to discussion and writing. In large classes, students can be asked periodically to turn to a neighbor and discuss a particular question. They can divide into groups for the same purpose or to read and respond to drafts of one another's papers. Even this limited approach to community can increase the comfort level of minority students. Teachers of large classes may find collaboration particularly advantageous because when students write collaboratively and receive the same grades on a particular project, teachers need grade fewer projects and can, thus, assign more writing. This is useful since generally the more students write and the more kinds of writing they do, the more expertise they feel and demonstrate.

Results

Students generally enjoy working in groups because the process helps them write better and because they feel less isolated. Retention rates have been excellent in my classes when I used frequent group work, and the same has been true for others using classroom collaboration (see Johnson, et al., 1991, for statistics). Since 1995, groups of entering students at my university have been clustered into various learning communities. Students travel together to at least three classes, all of which employ collaborative learning and keep the same base groups from class to class. Each year the group has grown; in fall 1998, approximately 500 entering students were clustered. About 70% of these students are Mexican American. In follow-up studies, students commented in interviews about how the groups helped them make friends and find study partners. One 18-year-old student said clustering "really does help because all your classes are with the same people. You work in groups. It establishes teamwork" (UTEP 2B). He also noted an increased sense of community, which he needed because he had no friends on campus when he arrived. He said, "I do feel more comfortable here because of the cluster classes" (UTEP 2B). Other students said they felt welcomed by members of their base groups as they entered the classroom, and instructors noted how students walked out of class chatting with members of their collaborative groups. In this way, the collaborative classroom expanded their social milieu, diminished feelings of isolation, and helped minority members identify with people from other ethnic/racial/gender groups. The term "learning community" is well chosen because its effect is, in general, to foster community development within the classroom.

Students seem to recognize that collaborative learning represents the university's attempt to help them do well. Hurtado (1992) notes that institutional "commitment to diversity may significantly improve minority student perceptions" (562) of campus racial climate; this may increase the likelihood of retention and graduation of Mexican Americans and other minority students. At the end of the 1996 semester, students at my campus responded to questionnaires about the collaborative learning program. Of the 100 students involved in experimental collaborative learning communities that year, 89 agreed that the community always or frequently provided an environment in which students felt free to express their ideas. Ninety-five of 100 students felt that every student had been encouraged to participate in class discussions and activities, and 95 also felt that these courses encouraged respect for everyone. Eighty-nine students believed collaboration promoted a desire to learn and think critically, and the same number felt collaborative learning "contributed to increasing the success of students like me."

These kinds of attitudes correlate with positive school experiences for these mainly Mexican American students. Learning communities continue to operate on the UTEP campus with generally positive outcomes. Students involved in the learning communities, initiative have consistently had higher grade-point averages and better retention rates than those who had not participated. William Torres, one of the top ten students graduating from UTEP in 2001, credits the cluster program for his success. He says, "I now look forward to the future because I carry with me a solid foundation" (Top 10). These results strengthen my belief that collaborative learning approaches can benefit Mexican American students in particular as well as today's ethnically and gender-diverse student populations in general.

NOTE

Terminology for identifying ethnicity is controversial. When asked to explain the difference between Hispanic, Latino/a, Chicano/a, and similar terms, my students came up with contradictory responses, which seems to suggest that terminology is based on regional preference. Many (though not all) agree that they are "people of color" and that anybody who is not "of color" is Anglo or white. I use white in this essay as a catchall for this category. I have chosen the term Mexican American as most accurate to describe my students, most of whom are of Mexican descent, but use the term Hispanic when speaking in general about people with ancestry in Spanish-speaking countries. I follow the convention of not capitalizing general descriptors, like black or white. I do not mean to suggest by the use of any term that all people of a particular group are the same. Instead, I hope to highlight the difference in useful ways rather than ignoring it or pretending that it has no importance.

WORKS CITED

Allport, G. *The Nature of Prejudice.* New York: Doubleday, 1954.

Bettelheim, B. "Individual and Mass Behavior in Extreme Situations. *Journal of Abnormal and Social Psychology*, 38, 417–52, 1943.

Carter, Thomas P., & Roberto D. Segura. *Mexican Americans in School: A Decade of Change.* New York: College Entrance Examination Board, 1979.

Clark, K. B. *Dark Ghetto: Dilemmas of Social Power.* New York: Harper & Row, 1965.

Fredericksen, Elaine. "Silence and the Nontraditional Writer." *Teaching English in the Two-Year College*, 25 (2), 115–21, May 1998.

Garcia-Vazquez, Enedina, Luis Vazquez, & Chi-Yu Huang. "Psychological Factors and Language: Impact on Mexican American Students." *The College Student Journal*, 32 (1), 6–18, March 1998.

Goodlad, John I., & Pamela Keating (Eds.). *Access to Knowledge: The Continuing Agenda for Our Nation's Schools.* New York: College Entrance Examination Board, 59–89, 1994.

Grier, W. H., & P. M. Coobs. *Black Rage.* New York: Basic Books, 1968.

"Hispanic Population Nears 30 Million." *El Paso Times*, Friday, August 7, 1998: 6A.

Holzman, Michael. "Observations on Literacy: Gender, Race and Class." In Richard Bullock and John Trimbur (Eds.). *The Politics of Writing Instruction: Post-Secondary.* (pp. 297–305). Portsmouth, NH: Boynton/Cook, 1991.

Horning, Alice S. "The 'Climate of Fear' in the Teaching of Writing." In C. L. Caywood, & G. R. Overing (Eds.). *Teaching Writing: Pedagogy, Gender, and Equity.* (pp. 65–79). Albany NY: State University of New York Press, 1987.

Hurtado, Sylvia. "The Campus Racial Climate:Contexts of Conflict." *Journal of Higher Education*, 65 (5), 539–69, September/October 1992.

Johnson, David W., Roger T. Johnson, Karl A. Smith. *Active Learning: Cooperation in the College Classroom.* Edina, MN: Interaction Book Co., 1991.

Kagan, Spencer. "Co-op Co-op: A Flexible Cooperative Learning Technique." In Slavin et al., 437–62.

————, G. Lawrence Zahn, Keith Widaman, Joseph Schwarzwald, & Gary Tyrrell. "Classroom Cultural Bias." In Slavin et al., 277–312, 1985.

Ogbu, John U. "Overcoming Racial Barriers to Equal Access." In Goodlad and Keating, 59–89.

Porter, O. F. *Undergraduate Completion and Persistence at Four-year Colleges and Universities.* Washington, DC: The National Institute of Independent Colleges and Universities, 1990.

Prendergast, Catherine. "Race: The Absent Presence in Composition Studies." *College English*, 50 (1), 36–53, September 1998.

Rendon, L. I. "Validating Culturally Diverse Students: Toward a New Model of Learning and Student Development. *Innovative Higher Education*, 19 (1), 33-51, 1994.

Sewell, W., & R. Hauser. "The Wisconsin Longitudinal Study of Social and Psychological Factors in Aspirations and Achievements." In A. Kerckhoff (Ed.), *Research in the Sociology of Education and Socialization.* Greenwich, CT: JAI Press, 1980.

Sharan, Shlomo. "Cooperative Learning and the Multiethnic Classroom." In Slavin et al., 255–76.

Sharan, Shlomo, Peter Kussell, Rachel Hertz-Lazarowitz, Yael Bejarano, Shulamit Raviv, and Yael Sharan. "Cooperative Learning Effects on Ethnic Relations and Achievement in Israeli Junior-High-school Classrooms." In Slavin et al.,313–44.

Slavin, Robert, Shlomo Sharan, Spencer Kagan, Rachel Hertz Lazarowitz, Clark Webb, Richard Schmuck. *Learning to Cooperate: Cooperating to Learn.* New York & London: Plenum Press, 1985.

Steele, Claude M. "A Threat in the Air: How Stereotypes Shape Intellectual Identity and Performance." *American Psychologist*, 52 (6), 613–29, June 1997.

"Study Says Latino Students Lag." *El Paso Times.* Wednesday, July 22, 1998: 4A.

Suarez, Shirley, Blaine Fowers, Carolyn Garwood, & Jose Szapocznik. "Biculturalism, Differentness, Loneliness, and Alienation in Hispanic

College Students." *Hispanic Journal of Behavioral Sciences*, 19 (4), 489–505, November 1997.

Tomlinson-Clarke, Saundra. "A Longitudinal Study of the Relationship between Academic Comfort, Occupational Orientation and Persistence Among African American, Hispanic and White College Students." *Journal of College Student Development*, 35, 25–34, January 1994.

"Top 10." *Horizons*, May 3, 2001: 4.

"UTEP Enrollment Falls." *El Paso Times.* Wednesday, September 16, 1998: 1A–2A.

CHAPTER FOUR
Evaluators: Teaching Writers to Assess Themselves

The process of grading student writing frustrates many dedicated educators. Reading, responding to, and grading student work takes up a large percentage of most teachers' time. Sometimes the process makes them angry with their students and themselves. Too often the process gives both teacher and student a sense of failure, even when the student receives a passing grade. These problems are exacerbated when students who enter a writing class already have fears about their abilities, when they are different from their teachers, and when they feel like outsiders in a system not designed to meet their specific needs and talents. Negotiated grading offers a positive response to this dilemma.

Negotiated grading involves student-teacher consensus rather than the standard procedure where teachers collect student writing, perhaps read and comment so that students can revise, and then assign a grade to the final draft. Students involved in grade negotiation write letters to instructors about individual essays and/or about their entire output, often in the form of an end-of-semester portfolio; they reflect on their work and do a self-evaluation based on some agreed-upon rubric or set of guidelines. Each student then suggests the grade he or she expects to receive and explains why in some depth. This gives students an opportunity to analyze their own strengths and weaknesses as writers and to consider the difficulties involved with assessment. Teachers then read (or reread) the selected essay(s) plus the student evaluation and agree or disagree with the suggested grade. If there is a wide discrepancy, it can be dealt with through individual conferences in which some sort of compromise is reached. This might, on occasion, require revision, submission of more student work, or calling in an outside reader. Student and teacher can also decide jointly on the method for reevaluating and reassigning a grade.

Theoretical Underpinnings

There is considerable theoretical support for this approach both from feminist and composition scholars. Feminist educator Frances Maher points to race, gender, and class as elements that complicate modern society and suggests the need for "classroom exercises in feminist pedagogy to help students and ourselves [educators] listen to and come to terms with our differences and the multiple capacities and social responsibilities within ourselves" (Inquiry, 192). Maher recommends "an interactive pedagogy" where students "grade themselves or are involved in the process by which criteria for grades are set " (Classroom, 45). Margaret McKenna emphasizes making "our campuses more humane, more collaborative, more welcoming to students of diverse ages, races and gender" (299) as vital to the feminist agenda. This attention to accepting and coming to terms with difference is a major underpinning of feminist approaches to education.

Student populations have rapidly moved away from the young, white, middle-class model that was envisioned in the early days of American schools. Yet most students today are graded by the same standards as were those one hundred years ago. The model paper is still logical, objective, organized, and correct in terms of standard American English. Most writing teachers are white, middle-class females brought up themselves in a tradition that values these attributes. They grade by this model, even in cases where they are not naturally drawn to that standard themselves. They have learned their lessons well, but feminist pedagogy aims to subvert these lessons and broaden the model to accept—even encourage—a more intuitive, subjective, circular approach to some writing. Feminists also allow space for non-standard (or foreign) language when that language conveys a special tone or achieves a special purpose. Negotiated grading fits in with this broader concept in that students have an opportunity to explain their divergence from the norm. Rather than judging student writing from their usual stance, teachers may be persuaded by student rhetoric to accept, enjoy, and reward variety.

Another precept of feminist pedagogy is the desire to reduce hierarchies and "to create pedagogical situations which empower students [and] demystify canonical knowledges" (Luke and Gore, 1). The grading process often takes on the qualities of mystery in students' eyes. When teachers fail to establish criteria and when they grade papers with few comments or merely accompanied, after the fact, by justification for low grades, students understandably wonder whether the process is designed to help or harm them. Certainly situations like this make them feel powerless. Few ever approach a teacher, especially at the postsecondary level, to ask how they could have done better. Some mumble to friends, but not many have the courage to challenge a grade.

Negotiated Grades

Negotiated grading, by contrast, gives students a feeling of control. I often ask my own students to write about negotiated grades. The following is a sample of their comments on negotiated grading of final portfolios:

> The idea of getting to help decide my final grade meant a lot to me. It showed that the teacher cared what I thought.

> I liked the idea of evaluating our work because I had some idea of how I was improving.

> I am glad to have some say in the final grading of my portfolio. Most teachers limit the amount of leverage a student is given, especially when grading papers. This process allowed me logically to understand why I earned a grade.

> Evaluating my own writing made me take a step back and judge my writing.

> It was nice having a teacher that would listen. I enjoyed being able to sit down and write, "Hey, I worked really hard on this."

> I did feel more secure with being able to offer an opinion about my grade. At midterm I was a little skeptical and didn't think that my opinion was going to matter, but after receiving my portfolio comments, I knew it had.

> The fact that I had some say in the final grading of my portfolio was wonderful. It was actually the aspect of the class I was most happy with.

It is rewarding for teachers when students like their practices, but even more telling in these comments (and they are standard for students engaged in negotiated grading) is the attention students focused on their own work. As they graded themselves, and again as they wrote about the grading process, they took time to reflect on themselves as writers and to recognize the progress they had made during the course of the semester. They also gained confidence in their ability to evaluate their own work. Most important of all is the apparent understanding that student voices matter, that they have some control over their outcomes.

Negotiated grades also move students away from the notion that the grade is everything and that students who get the highest grades are the most meritorious. Students from nontraditional backgrounds may despair of ever getting high grades because of second-language interference, poor reading skills, lack of equipment like computers with spell-check and grammar-check, lack of time due to family and work responsibilities, or a myriad of other reasons. They feel unable to compete, and, in many cases, their cultural background makes competition unsuitable for them. According to Catherine Lamb, negotiation and mediation change the goal of education, moving it from competition to cooperation. She says these approaches mean the objective "is no longer to win but to arrive at a solution in a just way that is acceptable to both sides" (18). Surely competition (or even perceived competition) between student and teacher can create anxiety and hostility. Much better a cooperative attitude toward grading wherein both parties seek to establish trust and to arrive at an evaluation that is fair and accurate in the eyes of everyone concerned (which in a school situation may include a hierarchy of other class members, colleagues, and administrators as well as the immediate parties).

Mediation involves a third person (or group of persons) in the decision-making process and may employ conflict resolution strategies. In cases where student and teacher disagree markedly about the excellence of a particular piece, another reader may be called upon to read the essay. This is best done blind—where the new reader has no idea of the grade preferred by either teacher or student. In cases of racial or cultural difference between student and teacher, the reader may be a member of the student's group to ensure fairness.

Many teachers and administrators wonder if students can really grade themselves fairly. They may celebrate deferred grading through the use of end-of-semester portfolios and still fear negotiated grades, worrying that teachers will be taken advantage of by unreasonable students or will disappoint unrealistic ones. But these fears prove unwarranted when students are well prepared for the grading task.

My own experience has been that most students grade themselves quite accurately if they have the opportunity to practice the process and if they have an understandable rubric to follow, preferably one they have had a hand in developing. After practice-grading anonymous sample essays in groups and individually, I require students to submit a cover letter for each of their own essays wherein they discuss and then evaluate each essay based on the form called "Guidelines for Evaluating Individual Essays" (see Appendix, Chapter 5). This rubric is merely a sample; it may be even better to use guidelines that students have helped to create. Students' self-evaluations usually coincide with mine to within half a grade, that is, the difference between B and B− or between B− and C+. This finding is corroborated by Bloom (1997) in her article "Why I (Used to) Hate to Give Grades," in which she says, "On the whole, my grades were about a half-step lower than the students', because of differences in emphasis. But because our points of agreement were so numerous, it was also easy to tell the students in person why (in most cases) they'd be getting some form of B instead of the A they desired, but didn't necessarily expect" (369). In years of practice, I have had only a few instances where a student seemed unrealistic about the quality of work. When this occurred, I had another instructor read the student's work without indicating to that reader how I had rated it or how the student had. I then discussed this outside evaluation with the student and offered the opportunity to speak with the second reader. Students tend to accept these joint opinions more readily than those coming from single graders.

The cover letters students write to accompany essays or portfolio pieces serve a number of important functions. They provide the major impetus for self-evaluation because each includes a verbalization of the process the writer goes through in evaluating the particular essay. Putting thoughts into words forces students to look again at the set of guidelines that were created or previously discussed and practiced in class. While the natural tendency would seem to lean toward giving themselves high grades because they worked hard or because considerable emotion went into the development of a piece, students who reexamine the guidelines must admit that hard work and emotion do not form part of the assessment procedure. On the other hand, the cover letter gives them a place to mention effort and personal attachment to the subject of the essay if they feel a desire to do so. Even when such mention makes no difference in grading, students enjoy the opportunity to tell about this part of their process.

The following excerpts from student letters suggest the self-reflection cover letters can elicit. About an individual essay, one student wrote the following:

> I chose to include this essay in my portfolio because of its tone. I feel that this is my best work due to its brisk and humorous tone and style. For me to write something humorous took a lot of work because I am usually quiet and serious...I learned a lot from this essay. I learned how to critique myself. I also learned how to revise a paper more than one time. Each time I went to revise, I found ways to improve it even more.

> I wrote four drafts of this paper. After reading the first, I noticed that it had a tendency to ramble. The thoughts were completely unorganized. Sentences were written clearer in the second version. Research was added to the third. This helped my argument seem stronger and more detailed, but for some reason I still wasn't satisfied. After reading over it numerous times, the problem finally came to me. It was the first and second paragraphs. The first had absolutely nothing to do with the topic I was discussing, so it was completely eliminated. The second was misplaced. I moved it to the end which made all the difference.

Some individual cover letters focus on specifics; others are more general. All demonstrate the process of self-reflection and consideration of the individual as a writer. This represents a significant change from students who look to the teacher to judge their work without recognizing their own responsibility for success or failure.

About the overall portfolio, students said the following:

STUDENT 1: Well, the semester is finally over, as you can probably tell by the signs of relief around campus. Personally, this new year has been a trying one, full of stress and worries. I know that I am glad that summer has finally come. From this semester, I would have to say that this English course was one of my most demanding classes, requiring continuous writing, the kind I was not used to. I am not the type of person that particularly enjoys writing for the fun of it, so if writing is an assignment, I honestly do not look forward to it. But when it comes to getting things done, I have no other choice but to do the best I possibly can. Failure is not a choice. Self-evaluating helped me realize just how much work my papers needed. I knew I needed to improve with each draft, and I honestly think I did.

STUDENT 2: I feel much better about submitting this essay for portfolio now than I did at mid-term. It has been through another series of extensive revisions. This time, I have reorganized the structure of most paragraphs by grouping ideas differently. For example, both the Central Park rapists and the Bobbits receive their own paragraphs at the beginning of the essay. This serves to grab readers' attention and makes it easier to connect the respective situations in subsequent paragraphs.

Previous versions of the essay seemed to leap between topics because my transitions were not adequate to guide the reader through the essay. Everything was connected, logical, and coherent to me but left the reader feeling a little lost. The new organization and addition of summarizing statements makes it easier for the reader to follow.

I also replaced the light, sarcastic tone with a serious one throughout the essay. My neighbor said the flippant tone made the essay seem weird and made me seem warped. Some subjects don't work with a casual style.

In spite of all the work I had already done on "Face the Music," I was still unhappy with it three days before the due date. I felt the essay was unfinished but did not know what was missing. I asked another friend to proofread it for me. She said that I needed to summarize my ideas at the end of the paper. There was no conclusion, no synopsis of my points. The essay just abruptly stopped. It sounds like an obvious flaw, and I don't know why I couldn't see it myself. I guess we occasionally need someone to point out the obvious. With the addition of the concluding paragraph, this essay is finally done.

Purpose	A–
Organization	B+
Details	B+
Voice/Tone	A
Mechanics	A
Overall Grade	A–

STUDENT 3: Submitted for your approval, or at least your opinion, is my final work in your class. I have to say, with all honesty, 'Thank God!' I don't want to give the impression that I have not enjoyed the class (I have), but writing continues to be very difficult for me. I have most definitely become a much better writer, but I find that this just means I expect more of myself and…wait a minute—I guess that's good.

STUDENT 4: The most difficult part of this letter is this section. I now have to decide what I think I have earned for this portfolio. I am not anywhere in the neighborhood of a Martin Luther King, Jr. but I do believe that this is an A– portfolio. I believe this for a few reasons. The points made by the essays are much more fully developed than they were before. The essays have demonstrated real growth between drafts rather than minor editing. I do believe that all of the errors from the mid-term portfolio have been corrected. Should I not receive the grade that I want, I can still rest at ease knowing that thanks to my ability to evaluate my own work I haven't received anything less than an A on any paper I have written in my other classes since the fifth week of this semester.

Cover letters are vitally important because they add the element of reflection to the writing process (Yancey, 1992). They allow students to consider how much they learn from their successes, and also how much small failures teach. Asking students to submit all preliminary drafts along with their final drafts and cover letter often causes students to reread the drafts and to consider how much their writing has improved.

In my experience, student reaction to negotiated grading is generally enthusiastic. The major objections have to do with initial insecurity, mainly caused by inexperience with self-evaluation. Their previous school experience has accustomed these students to immediate teacher feedback and to strong teacher control of both writing and grading, so they undervalue their own abilities to critique themselves. Giving a midterm negotiated grade allows students to practice the technique and makes them more comfortable with the process. By the end of the semester, most students vigorously support negotiated grading and advocate its use in other classes. The following are typical comments:

> I liked being able to write my thoughts down and contributing to the decision of the final grade.

> The idea of getting to help decide my final grade meant a lot to me. It showed that the teacher cared what I thought.

> I did not think I could evaluate myself as a writer or as a student. Knowing that I now can has helped me understand the writing process.

> I feel comfortable criticizing and evaluating my work now that I know what elements to look for.

The self-assessment process requires considerable effort on the part of teacher and students because it represents a distinct change from the norm. The major difficulty for students seems to be the lack of accustomed feedback in the form of grades. They must learn to read teacher suggestions but worry less about "what the teacher wants." Based on classrooms, experience, practice, and peer response, students can decide for themselves what makes a particular piece of writing successful.

Teachers can help students see that they are able, within a certain agreed-upon framework, to determine for themselves the shape of an essay. Students can write what they want and still receive high marks. For their part, students must learn to deal with a higher-than-normal level of anxiety, at least until midterm. Usually once they have negotiated their midterm grade—even if they have not been totally successful—they feel more confident about their abilities to judge their own work and achieve the final grade they hope for. My experience suggests that students in negotiated grading situations work much harder after midterm than before and much harder than students in classes where grades are not negotiated. I think this is because they have gotten the idea that they are working for themselves, aiming for standards that they clearly understand and feel confident they can meet. They know they are not in competition with classmates for a few top grades, and they do not have to rely on an instructor's mysterious decisions. Grading guidelines give them focus and support.

Negotiated grading is not trouble free. A number of students resist this approach, struggle, and fail. Some take self-assessment lightly, figuring the teacher will really do the grading anyway. When teachers do the grading, students have a constant prod to keep them moving forward. The grade prod does not have the same effect when students negotiate grades. I have designed approaches to deal with this problem. Although not always successful, these approaches do help many students.

One strategy I use to prevent low grades is copious use of positive marginal comments. I link this to another strategy—dividing content revision and proofreading into separate and distinct steps. Trained by my early experiences as student then teacher, I found this a difficult transition. For a long time, I felt guilty if I did not mark every single error on every single paper. Reading composition theorists (see Anson) and attending sessions on assessment at professional conferences reinforced my intuitive feeling that students revise more willingly with positive rather than negative reinforcement. I now attempt to comment only on content in early drafts, often phrasing my comments as questions that ask for clarification, additional information, details, examples, etc. I tell students what confuses me and what I, as reader, need to clear up my confusion. I make a real effort to tell students what I like about their writing and what they may want to do more of. I am never as good at this as I want to be. Time presses. Life interferes. But I believe that the better I do at commenting, the greater success my students experience.

My students and I disregard mechanics on the first few drafts except in cases where error interferes with understanding. Even then, we ask questions about the content (Did you mean to say this or that?) rather than focusing on the mechanical problem. When writers revise to clarify, errors often disappear. It is important for teachers to model these techniques by commenting on students' first writing samples and by providing opportunities for students to practice together responding to the writing of someone not known to them. Then when they move to peer response groups, their responses are positive and useful.

Mechanics certainly do matter in our society, and my students handle the task of polishing usage and style in proofreading circles. When students have next-to-final drafts ready, they form a circle and pass their papers clockwise. The recipient reads and comments in the margin, in pencil, on perceived errors (Do you need a comma in this sentence? Check spelling of *judgment*). When finished with one piece, the student passes the paper to the next available reader in the circle. This person also comments in the margin. When each essay has been read by four or five people, it is returned to the owner who may then request clarification from other students or the teacher. Everyone accepts that comments are suggestions that may, in fact, be less appropriate than the original. It is up to the writers to check for best choices as they work on their final revisions. When they evaluate their final drafts for a grade, students should have a good idea of how to rate themselves on this part of the rubric. My students tell me they like proofreading circles and find them extremely useful both in helping them turn out a correct finished product and in gaining confidence about the mechanical part of the writing process.

Student-teacher conferences provide the best possible feedback to students learning about self-assessment. I schedule at least two mandatory conferences per semester, but also meet individually with students for mini-conferences (five to ten minutes) when they are workshopping or doing group work. I also encourage them to visit me outside of class or to make use of any available tutoring services. If none are available, they can consult with a friend or parent who has some expertise.

Conclusion

Would it be better to grade an occasional essay without the negotiation process? I have considered this frequently but always decide that students would not benefit from this departure from negotiated grades. Their task is to see and evaluate themselves as writers rather than as students who get judged by a teacher. I want the power to be theirs, even though they sometimes have trouble learning to wield it.

Most writing teachers now emphasize revision. Many use portfolio assessment. In my experience, however, few have ventured into negotiated grading. I would like to suggest experimenting with it because my students and I agree that it works. It adds a valuable dimension to deferred grading, emphasizing the reflection process and arming students for future writing situations where revision is not required but remains necessary for optimal achievement.

WORKS CITED

Anson, Chris (Ed.). *Writing and Response: Theory, Practice, and Research.* Urbana, IL: NCTE, 1989.

Black, Laurel, D. Daiker, J. Sommers, and G. Stygall (Eds.). *New Directions in Portfolio Assessment.* Portsmouth, NH: Heinemann, 1994.

Bloom, Lynn Z. "Why I (Used to) Hate to Give Grades." *College Composition and Communication,* 48.3, 360–71, October 1997.

Lamb, Catherine E. "Beyond Argument in Feminist Composition." *College Composition and Communication,* 42 (1), 11–24, February 1991.

Luke, Carmen, & Jennifer Gore. *Feminisms and Critical Pedagogy.* New York: Routledge, 1992.

Maher, Frances A. "Classroom Pedagogy and the New Scholarship on Women." In Margo Culley and Catherine Portuges (Eds.). *Gendered Subjects: The Dynamics of Feminist Teaching.* Boston: Routledge, 1985. (pp. 29–48).

———. "Inquiry Teaching and Feminist Pedagogy." *Social Education,* 15, 186–8, 190–2, March 1987.

McKenna, Margaret A. "Shaping the Change: The Need for a New Culture in Higher Education." In Joyce Antler and Sari Knopp Biklen (Eds.). *Changing Education: Women as Radicals and Conservators* (pp.295–301). New York: State of New York Press, 1990.

Yancey, Kathleen (Ed.). *Portfolios in the Writing Classroom: An Introduction.* Urbana, IL: NCTE, 1992.

CHAPTER FIVE
Extenders: Helping Young Writers Enter the Academy

In the March 1996 edition of *College English,* Richard E. Miller complains about the "rift between the personal and the academic" that his reading has not prepared him to heal or "at least to build a bridge across its seemingly expansive divide" (267). Miller seeks ways to help his students "hear what I, as a representative of the academy, am saying" and learn "how to speak, read, and write in ways that I can hear" (283). He knows the gap between private and public that annoys seasoned writers can create havoc in the composition classroom. As they advance in high school and move to college, student writers struggle to clarify their thoughts and develop a unique voice[1] at the same time they attempt to learn the language of the academy. Because they do not feel comfortable with the barrage of new material, new styles, and new vocabulary, students may distrust their own ideas and their ability to write about these ideas and may have trouble claiming authority over their own academic output. Typical of most students learning to write, these problems are magnified when young writers come from homes where English is a second language and/or where they do not have consistent access to academic books and language from an early age. Writers thrust into academic settings may feel frustrated. They may harbor anger against teachers whom they perceive are trying to steal their authenticity by expecting them to use forms, vocabulary, and styles that do not come naturally.

Theories of Resistance

Most educators begin their careers with great hope and optimism, assuming that they have something to give to students that students need. From their college-graduate, adult perspective, they see clearly that students must enter the world of academics and learn to speak its language before they can be successfully educated. It comes as a great shock to them to discover that students may resist what they have to offer. Frequently they blame this resistance on personal obstinacy or laziness. Theory explains, however, that resistance has complex underpinnings related to culture, class, and race. Teachers cannot lead students into the academy without a clear understanding of these basic elements.

Cultural theorists like Henry Giroux and Paulo Freire show that "resistance is more than willful ignorance or dysfunctional behavior. Instead, it is a means by which people respond to the constraints of social and educational structures" (Ritchie, 1). These theorists call into question the commonplace image of America as a melting pot into which all citizens wish to be assimilated. They recognize instead that to many nontraditional students, both native-born and immigrant, assimilation means a loss of culture, of language, of the differences that make them unique. Critical pedagogy calls for dismantling old notions about assimilation and adopting a new transformative approach to teaching in which students are shown how academic reading and writing can relate to their lives. Giroux says that teachers and students should function as intellectuals working together to create their own brand of truth.

Feminist theorists (Belenky et al., Bem, Epstein, Flynn, Lewis, Maher, and others) also argue against pedagogies of assimilation, disputing that no schooling can be neutral. They abhor traditional methods of education that cater to a white, male, middle-class model and are inappropriate for women and other previously disenfranchised minorities. Feminists encourage a radical pedagogy where standard discourse conventions present grounds for confrontation and change. They argue that minority voices have been silenced too long and that minority populations require new teaching methodologies where students have a certain latitude in what they read and how they respond to and write about it.

The approach suggested in this chapter, working from personal response and moving gradually to academic expression of these personal ideas, aims to engage students and teachers in this kind of transformative process.

Theories of Ownership

Young writers frequently lack what has been called "personal authority," also referred to as "ownership" and discussed in various contexts by many composition theorists (Adler-Kassner, 1998; Brannon & Knoblauch, 1984; Carroll, 1991; Phelps, 1989; Schwegler, 1991; Spigelman, 1998). Linda Adler-Kassner, for example, suggests that personal authority or ownership is that which ensures students' finding "some of their own literacies and values" reflected in their writing (225), but Robert Schwegler wonders how much authority students can attain in a classroom where teachers make and grade writing assignments. Louise Wetherbee Phelps suggests that the paradigm of ownership is undergoing a shift, moving away from the Romantic notion of a single owner toward shared authority.

This shift often creates a tension between the apparent binaries of collaboration and ownership with some students unsure about what is really theirs in the finished product. Students particularly express discontent when they are asked to write together and receive a shared grade for the product. They complain that some students work more than others and that the results do not belong to them. They also dislike having others, especially teachers, forcing changes in style or content, saying, "That's not really what I wanted to say. The teacher wants me to sound just like her." This may be particularly painful for students who already feel marginalized and question the value of their own output.

Bruce Horner writes about a different kind of binary, that of author versus student writer. He examines the work of a number of composition theorists (Bartholomae, Ede, Elbow, Lu, Lunsford, and others) and concludes that these binaries can be joined through a concerted effort of teacher and students working together "to investigate writing as a social and material practice, confronting and revising those practices that have served to reify the activity of writing into texts and authorship" (526). My interpretation of this suggestion is that students can become "authors" only gradually and only through the act of writing, but they will be successful in this only insofar as their teachers acknowledge what they bring to the task. What they produce must always depend on what they know, and this is a combination of their academic reading and their personal interactions in the world.

Discourse Conventions and the Plight of the Nontraditional Student

In an atmosphere where even experts cannot come to a conclusive definition, college students must somehow move from personal ownership of their writing to what might be called academic authority, that is, ownership of their academic voice or voices. They need assistance to do this and some clear direction. I believe it is not enough for students to recognize their own cultural milieu in the writing, or to say, "I wrote this," or to feel possessive about their product to the point where they refuse to change any of it. In my view, authority is more than a willingness to put one's name on the writing; it is a matter of well-founded confidence based on meeting specific guidelines. When writers feel sure they have presented an intelligent, carefully crafted piece in a style appropriate to the intended (in this case, academic) audience, they are truly ready to claim ownership over the writing.

Unfortunately, beginning writers have special difficulties in this area for several reasons. First, as Gesa Kirsch points out in *Women Writing the Academy*, "part of *having* authority entails being *perceived* as an authority" (49). Kirsch refers specifically to female academics, but her comments pertain equally well to beginning writers who are generally perceived by faculty members and others to lack authority on all subjects other than personal narratives or simple how-to essays. A 1994 study by Ann Penrose and Cheryl Geisler supports the notion that college students need experience to feel confident. The study compares the writing of a doctoral student with that of a college freshman and suggests to the researchers that students write better when they believe "that there is authority to spare—that there is room for many voices" (517). They write more and better when they trust themselves and feel they have something valuable to contribute.

In addition to being perceived as poor writers and thinkers, students also perceive themselves as lacking in necessary skills, language, and authority. They fear that what they write will not be acceptable, that others write better than they, that they have nothing valuable to write. Carol Lea Clark asked groups of her entering composition students why they do not think of themselves as writers, and they answered, "We're not good enough…famous enough…creative enough…What we write doesn't count" (218). Some of my own students reflected on how they felt at the beginning of a first-year college writing course, and the following represents some of their comments:

> One of the biggest fears an incoming freshman has is that his or her writing skills are not at a high enough standard to compete in a college curriculum.

> I thought I was an awful writer.

> I was worried that my writing would not be as good as other people in my class.

> I was apprehensive about beginning a college-level English course.

These worries seem to affect most first-year college writers and to have added impact on students who already feel marginalized, as in the case of physically handicapped class members, students from lower-class families, and members of ethnic minorities. Sometimes such fears result in difficult starts, occasionally even paralysis. Students hesitate to write because they fear that they cannot do so successfully; they worry most of all about academic writing and their belief that they do not know enough to do a good job.

If they hope to be perceived as knowledgeable in the advanced writing community, students must learn academic language, but David Bartholomae and others have shown that this learning does not come easily or quickly. And at the same time they struggle to acquire the proper vocabulary, student writers must learn to assume an academic stance toward a given subject, to write objectively and with some degree of sophistication. Authority also requires the proper use of academic conventions like citation methods and smooth incorporation of quotations from other sources into the new text.

All students have some difficulty learning to use these discourse conventions; to nontraditional students, they represent a challenge on multiple fronts because these students often resent standards that do not seem to relate to them. Even unsophisticated students, who cannot articulate their resistance, may recognize that academic conventions are based on a white, middle-class standard. The language of the academy does not sound like the home language of most students; it is especially alien to those who have few books in the home or whose books are written in a different language. If they do not know consciously, their unconscious tells them that standards are about power. The current system that emphasizes form and correctness instills fear and anger in students who may well ask themselves, "Whose standard is this anyway? How can I measure up to a standard I don't recognize? Why should I conform to conventions that have nothing to do with my life?" A transformational pedagogy does not ignore conventions. It considers the epistemology—the origins, nature, methods, and limits of knowledge—that students bring to the classroom. It allows them their comfort zone and recognizes their literacies, letting them tell their stories. Rather than imposing academic standards with a harsh hand or ignoring them completely, teachers may choose to set them aside temporarily in favor of an exchange of ideas. By concentrating initially on personal response and critical thinking about important and relevant issues, teachers can give students space to explore and experience the academy. Once they have built some confidence, they can discuss academic writing and decide together how to move toward the model that will allow them to be heard. They can confront their own marginalization and determine what they need to do to gain acceptance to a community that can benefit from what they have to say.

A Plan of Action

I propose that composition teachers can help beginning academic writers gain a sense of their own authority by asking first for personal response to an issue and then guiding students, in a series of graduated steps, toward public (academic) writing. This is certainly not a new idea. Most writing instructors begin the semester with expressive writing that is based on students' personal experience and expresses their personal feelings and beliefs. Often presented as first-person narratives, these essays have considerable benefit in that they authorize first-year writers as knowledgeable, if only within their personal sphere. These essays do not usually require academic language or sophisticated conventions and often result in the good grades students recognize as marks of success. Unfortunately, these positive beginnings tend to be short-lived. Subsequent assignments generally move quickly to strictly academic forms, often termed "public writing," wherein personal experience is perceived as having little value, and outside sources become the best authority. Students get the message that what they think no longer counts, that the important opinions come from the professor and from outside authors. Ownership moves from "mine" to "theirs" as student writers cede authority to others.

The method I have been experimenting with for several years in my first-year composition courses differs from that described above in that it requires students to develop *the same piece of writing* from personal to public through a regulated series of multiple drafts. Final drafts are evaluated cooperatively by the student writer and the instructor *using an established rubric* against which the final draft is measured. This chapter demonstrates the process in two students, one white American female of traditional age (18–24) who was completing a first-semester composition class, and the other, a Mexican woman, also of traditional age, enrolled in a second-semester composition class. These students' essays were selected because drafts were available for each from the first in-class writing through completion and also because I was able to obtain information about their continued success as college writers. Karen and Marisol have graciously allowed me to use their work in its original, unedited form. The progress shown in their drafts is typical of most students taught by this method.

The classes from which these essays emerged were both geared toward an end-of-semester portfolio that constituted 50% of the final grade. No essay received an individual grade, and grading of the entire portfolio was deferred until the last weeks of the semester. This allowed students to produce as many revisions of a given essay as they wished or had time to complete. Drafts went through peer-response groups, and at least one draft was reviewed by the instructor and discussed in a one-to-one conference. Students could request additional conferences on subsequent drafts and/or consult learning-center tutors.

Initial personal responses resulted from reading essays, stories, or articles. Each reading led to class discussion and an in-class writing period lasting from ten to thirty minutes. These "essay starts" were filed, unread, in individual student folders until a number (usually four or five) had accumulated. Each student then selected one "start" to develop further. After reading and discussing an article about a homeless gang member, Karen wrote the following:

Thesis: Struggle with poverty in the American family often results in the deterioration of family values.

The homeless, the starving, the abused, the abusers.... These are words that flash through our minds in bold print when we think about poverty in our "land of the free." Some people might say, "Yeah, welfare is free...for them." Decade after decade, Americans portray the underpriviledged persons their own nation as lazy and worthless. Many people may have this idea because the ones who live in poverty commit the most crimes. Have you ever thought about why they commit the crimes, though? Maybe it's because they need to steal to survive, maybe children have been raised to be criminals like their parents and they know of no other way to live.

Instructed to respond personally to the reading and discussion, Karen selects her particular area of interest: poverty and its relationship to crime. However, she begins with a formal thesis statement not requested by the instructor and cites "some people," "Americans," and "many people" as sources rather than asserting her own authority. As she composes, she displays an awareness of public writing, using plural rather than singular first person and later moving to second person as if to involve her audience. Like many first-year college writers, Karen brings with her some experiences from high school that make her uncomfortable with the personal voice even in situations where a personal response has been requested. She seems unsure of her own place as knowledge provider and seeks other "authorities" instead.

In this quickly written, informal "essay start," thoughts appear rather random. Because their time is severely limited, students can give little attention to organization or polish at this stage; in fact, students are instructed not to worry about correctness until later drafts. Instead Karen writes to develop the kernel of an idea. She later selects this piece for expansion because the topic continues to interest her.

Marisol's "essay start" responds to a selection, "The Mind of the Chimpanzee,' from Jane Goodal's book *Through a Window* (1990) and to class discussion of the selection. She writes:

I don't have any doubt in my mind that chimpanzees are intelligent. I believe that they can express anger, sorrow, happiness, and love. However, they aren't the only one. Most animals, especially mamals, have the ability to feel and give love. Many females protect and take care of their babyes until they saw they can protect themselves. Another thing from why I'm saying this is that I had have many pets and they have show me that they can love. For example, my five-weeks-old puppie expresses himself in many different ways. As fast as he hears the refrigitator door open he starts to bark and move his tale as showing me he knows is time to have a little milk. Also, he recognize my mood by hearing my voice. When I talk to him softly, it doesn't matter what I say, he starts to roll over and play. I'm sure he knows I want to play with him. Also, when he hears a strong and sharp voice, he automaticcilly hides himself as knowing he has have done something bad.

This paragraph moves quickly from Goodal's text to Marisol's personal experience; however, it also shows an awareness of audience. In the sentences which begin "Most animals..." and "Many females..." for instance, the writer clearly recognizes that others (academic others?) may read what has been written. Again, the text is unedited and quickly composed with obvious evidence of second-language interference, but Marisol, a second-semester student, seems immediately willing to validate her assertions with examples from her own life.

Each of these writers has a sense that so-called personal writing is not so personal in the college setting. This sense—discussed and experimented with during various class exercises focusing on audience, voice, and style—conveniently leads writers to the next step: the expanded essay.

In addition to students reading, discussing, and doing their short in-class writing, I devote some class time each day (my classes are generally taught two days a week and last an hour and twenty minutes) to studying topics like point of view, word choice, consistency of tense, topic sentence formation, thesis and paragraph development, and so forth. I may, for example, explain the concept of point of view and ask students to review previous readings to determine the point of view used in each. Students also consider why authors might have made certain choices for that particular piece. Exercises like this help prepare writers to expand their essay starts into more finished second drafts.

Second drafts can create unanticipated problems for beginning writers. While some students move quickly forward in developing their ideas, many get off track or bogged down in trivia. Some feel unable to complete an entire essay at this point. In my experience, this is generally the most chaotic step of the process. When some instructors first try revision, they make the mistake of allowing only two drafts, thus exacerbating rather than relieving writing problems. For me, the key to success is requiring (not merely requesting) a third draft because this is where I see the greatest progress for most young writers (and often in my own writing as well).

Because second drafts require considerable attention, I usually review them myself for the first essay of the semester. Third drafts go to peer-response groups. This works well because students have already read on their own papers the types of positive, content-oriented comments I encourage them to offer their fellow writers. This modeling seems to help them when they are called upon to give feedback to their peers, but both teachers and students need practice to develop commenting style. Articles on responding to student texts by Robert Connors and Andrea Lunsford and by Richard Straub have been particularly useful to me as has Chris Anson's *Writing and Response: Theory, Practice, and Research.* Connors and Lunsford, for example, discuss the advantage of "comments that reflected commitment to students and to learning" and praise "lengthy comments from teachers who seemed really to care, not only about students' writing, but also about the students themselves" (215). Students who read these kinds of comments on their own essays are more likely to write long, caring comments on the essays of their classmates. They are also more likely to direct attention to content rather than correctness and to comment on what they like rather than what they dislike.

One paragraph from a draft of Marisol's essay argued that humans are more intelligent than animals because humans "think, analyze, and choose the best answer to a problem." To illustrate this, Marisol wrote, "For instance, a teenager will not eat a rock even if someone insists him or demands him to do it. He/she has learn that a rock it's not food. He/she analyzed the question, and he decides for himself that eating a rock is not healthy." My comment on this section of the draft said, "I don't find this example convincing. Animals don't eat rocks either. I'd be more impressed, for example, by the fact that humans build shelters or design umbrellas to stay dry." On the next draft, Marisol uses a different example: "For instance, on a cloudy morning, it is common to see a man taking his jacket, umbrella, and coffee in hand when leaving his house. He knows that without his coat and umbrella, he may get wet, which may get him a cold. He understands the consequences of his acts, analyzes, and chooses."

Marisol also revises based on comments from other students. One suggests "You can change your title to a more specific one that could bring more interest to the reader," and Marisol changes from "An Issue of Nature" to the more specific (if less grammatical) "Animals' Intelligence: Are Theirs like Humans'?" Another student compliments Marisol's "good information and good usage of vocabulary, just need to give more examples and explanations about the monkeys' intelligence," and Marisol's next draft reflects her attempts to do this.

After students have had sufficient practice with the response process, second drafts may go through peer review while third drafts go to the instructor. I encourage students to take later drafts to tutors at our campus Teaching and Learning Center to work on style and polish. It might seem to someone not involved in the process that so much feedback from others would leave the writer wondering if the essay is still hers, but at every step the author makes her own choices. She accepts or rejects advice or adapts it in her own way just as Marisol rejected the idea of *designing* an umbrella and instead talked about the man's choice to *carry* one on a cloudy day. Students confronted with suggestions about a particular part of an essay may ignore the suggestions, make the suggested changes, make different changes, or, on occasion, omit or rewrite the entire concept. These choices seem to increase rather than decrease the author's sense of ownership. In a sense, the essay moves from "mine" (personal response) to "ours" (peer response) to "theirs" (outside research) and finally becomes "mine" again as each student shapes the multiple input into a unique essay.

As I already mentioned, second drafts often create the greatest difficulties for writers and require special attention. The second draft of Karen's poverty essay demonstrates the chaotic stage. It is important to note that this is her first attempt to expand an essay in her first college writing course. The difficulties she encounters reflect typical second-draft obstacles and indicate the importance of allowing students additional opportunities for revision.

Karen's Second Draft

Poverty: An Issue Facing American Families

The homeless...the starving...the abused...the abusers...These are pictures that flash through our minds when we think about poverty in the United States. However, there is more to poverty than we can see with our observant eyes. Every year, thousands of families divide, whether through divorce, separation, or custody battles, over financial problems. Also, families not receiving adequate health care and lacking proper nutrition and shelter are suffering and dying from serious illnesses. These persistent problems in our society illustrate how the struggle with poverty can become a main factor in the deterioration of the family.

Continuing decade after decade in our "Land of the Free," we Americans portray those who are poor as lazy, and therefore, we show little pity towards them. Some of us might even say, "Yeah, welfare is free... for them. The generation of this idea stems from the fact that many crimes are committed by individuals with little or no income. Most judgemental people, however, have not thought about why these crimes continue to occur in our country.

In the earliest years, as opposed to now, crime was almost unheard of, or even scarce in some places. However, now, the rapid growth of the crime rate is an indicator that some solution to this problem needs to be found. We can easily observe that in previous decades, as well as the present, humans committed crimes for the purpose of self satisfaction. If the poor are committing crimes, then what are they trying to satisfy? Maybe they have to steal just to survive…maybe they are unaware that there are people who can help them…or maybe children are being raised as criminals like their parents, and they know of no other way to live. After all, the crime rate is continuing to steadily incline.

Quite possibly, the corruption in our nation can be halted and eventually put to an end with the reconstruction of the family. Obviously, every family cannot live as harmoniously as The Brady Bunch. One reason is because the extent of problems within a family depends on that family's income. For instance, if a poor child sees schoolmates with nicer clothes and material possessions, he/she might do one of the following things: 1) If he/she saw a parent steal to achieve satisfaction, he/she would probably steal as well. 2) If he/she had been raised by honest parents, he/she would either be satisfied without the possessions or would find a way to acquire them honestly.

Evidently poverty is disintegrating the moral values of the family, as we continue to see the harsh reality of today's inner-city life. We, as a society, can do our part by continuing to educate, care for, and communicate with those living in poverty, instead of judging, shunning, and being too lazy, ourselves, to help them.

This second draft is just the sort to make writing teachers throw their hands up in despair if they forget to look back at the first draft and notice progress or if they forget that this is only an intermediate step toward a final product. In fact, this draft goes much farther than the "essay start" in articulating the writer's purpose—a call for more affluent members of society to acknowledge and attempt to ameliorate problems associated with children living in poverty. Teacher comments on this particular draft were sparse, calling for a conference leading to extensive revision rather than trying to "fix" what the teacher considers "mistakes."

In preparation for conferencing, class lessons during this period often focus on narrowing essay topics and presenting logical argument through the elimination of fallacies and through the compilation of a convincing and substantial body of evidence. Between the second and third drafts, students may or may not (depending on subject, availability of resources, and other factors) be encouraged to do research to strengthen their expertise on their chosen topic.

Following the advice of Muriel Harris and others, I generally try (and it is not always easy because I have to battle previous training and experience) to take a hands-off approach during student-teacher conferences, allowing the student to make changes on her draft if she feels inclined to do so but refraining from writing anything on the draft myself. I do this for several reasons. In learning the difference between editing and revising, students should be directed away from old drafts toward fresh ones that rely only loosely on what they have previously written. Also, and most importantly in terms of developing authority, I believe that teachers should be extremely careful not to usurp control over the essay. Once an instructor writes something on a student paper, the tendency for the student is to avoid changing those words or that section because she feels teacher knows best. This undermines the revision process and interferes with a student's ability to assume ownership of the finished product.

During our conference for her first essay, Karen began to focus on and discuss her purpose—to alert readers to the special educational needs of poor children. She discovered a need to narrow her scope and strengthen the organization of her essay. With this in mind, she constructed an outline and planned research to help her move from generalities to specifics. Reading professional articles helped Karen become acquainted with the way other writers had approached the subject and provided both information and a variety of models. These assisted in her composition of another, more informed draft, which she then submitted to a peer-response group. The group helped Karen gain a sense of audience. The interest of her peers encouraged her, as did a sense that she had information to impart. With peer comments and questions in mind, she revised once more and then brought her draft to a class proofreading session designed to eliminate surface error. Somewhere in this process, she let her original opening go; this may seem like a minor occurrence but represents to me a big change because it shows that the young author has opted for true revision rather than editing.

Karen evaluated her near-final draft by comparing it with a list of guidelines that had been handed out, discussed, and practiced early in the semester (included as Appendix D). As part of her final portfolio cover letter, she explained how she had evaluated the essay and what grade she thought each essay and the entire portfolio should receive.

Karen's final draft—not perfect, but much improved and written with noticeably more authority—appears as Appendix A. Her progress in developing a poorly articulated, nonauthoritative response to a research essay she then feels proud to include in her portfolio represents a great deal of effort and many pages of writing—much of which does not appear in her final draft. She credits her improvement to the opportunity for multiple drafting. This opportunity was accompanied by a gradual move from private to public writing, from personal to academic.

Teachers sometimes doubt that first-year writers recognize changes in their own writing, but my study indicates that they do. This is illustrated in Karen's final class reflection that includes the following:

> Over the past semester, I have observed that my writing has tremendously changed. Instead of looking for broad topics to research, I now look for more interesting, specific topics. This makes the actual research for documented papers more enjoyable and more of a challenge... As a writer, I feel that I have recently developed strength in holding the reader's attention. In the past, I wrote essays that were only opinionated. I have found that I sometimes wrote only to please myself, without regard to what the reader might feel. Through direction from my professor and countless revisions of my essays, I have become incredibly careful about the ideas that I put into my work. Another strength is my invitation to criticism. Each time I allow someone to read my papers, I ask them to help me make the papers better. This has proven beneficial every time.

Karen's response is not unique. In classes that emphasize multiple drafts and a gradual move from expressive to academic within the individual essay, most students say they come away from the experience feeling stronger about their writing. They claim a greater degree of ownership over their finished portfolios than students I have previously taught using single drafts and where I separated personal and academic essay writing.

The most important change this process elicits is the way students feel about their own abilities to think through a problem and express themselves in writing. By the end of the semester, Karen was able to write, "Overall, I do not think that I could have asked for a better learning experience. I have matured in my writing and I am entirely ready for English 102." Her confidence was justified. Karen received an *A* in second-semester composition, taught by a different instructor. She went on to complete two more English classes in which she also earned *A*s. Excellent grades in other classes that included a writing component attest to her continuing progress as an academic writer. In fact, the only grade lower than *A* in Karen's next two years of college was a *B* in chemistry, a nonwriting course.

Marisol's essay followed a slightly different pattern from initial in-class response to finished product. Her second and third drafts show steady progress from kernel to well-developed idea, but neither represents a finished essay. Perhaps because this was her second semester in a writing class, she produced an unfinished rather than what I would call a chaotic second draft. However, in these drafts her purpose remains unclear because she spends so much time on specific examples that she never gets to her overall thesis. Unlike Karen, Marisol also has to contend with typical problems of second-language students. Having spoken English for only three years, she needs extra help with usage, word choice, and style. These problems are illustrated in the following draft (number 3):

Marisol's Third Draft

An Issue of Nature

There is no doubt in my mind that some animals can feel anger, love, sadness, happiness, fear, and that they have enough intelligence to learn new things. However, animal intelligence would never been as human. Special intelligence stand out in animals such as chimpanzees and dogs.

Dogs, for instance, are known as the men's best friend for their ability to fulfill almost every owner necessity. A good example of this is my seven-weeks-old puppy named Toby. His a beige Chow chow puppy hyper enough to destroy an entire city. he likes to bite everything, except his new chewable toy of course, and to feel how its jaws converted them into pieces. Also, it seems as if he enjoys to wake me up at night. As soon as he wakes up, around 4:00 A.M., the party starts. It has not been a night that Toby hasn't growl, cry, and bark as inviting me to his party under the stars. Toby's lively and bright personality has always been in it; however, now he's starting to learn how to control it. Now, the puppy seems to understand when someone corrects him or praise him. As soon as he hears a strong sharp voice calling at him, he hides his tail between his legs and downs his ears. In the other hand, when the word Toby is said in a soft kind voice the puppy's whole body starts shaking with excitement.

The same thing happens with chimpanzees. They also have the ability to learn and to express what they feel. A great example is in James Goodal's story The Mind of the Chimpanzee. In this story Goodal mentions how Lucy, an eight year old chimpanzee, learn to communicate herself trough the American Sign Language. Thanks to this language Lucy was able to express her thoughts. If she wanted something, she made the hand movement necessary to express This is Lucy's.

The extraordinary ability chimpanzees have does not ends with Lucy's example. Washoe a highly intelligent chimpanzee, also mentioned in Goodal's story, takes Lucy's accomplishment one step further. Washoe did not only learned the ASL signs, but she taught them to her little pupil Loulis.

So, What is then the difference between animal's and human's intelligence? In Toby's case, learning it has been encouraged in part by memories of continuous situations. What I mean by this is that every time Toby did something wrong I have called him with a strong voice and scolded him a little slap. Or when I have played with him, I have used a soft voice and give him a treat. I understand that he has also learned some things by his own like to eat or clean himself, but that can be called and instinct of supervivence—if he does not eat, he dies. Toby has learned by repetition, by instinct, by supervivience, or by scolding or rewarding him. It is not like if the puppy awakes one morning and decides to learn a new trick.

Chimpanzees on the other hand, their learning has been encouraged by humans, nature or other animals. There is no doubt that chimpanzees are intelligent that they can make tools, solve simple problems, communicate, and teach. However, they do not have the necessity of knowledge humans have.

In spite of obvious errors, the reader observes here the emergence of a distinct, intelligent voice and an apparent sense of humor. This draft was followed by a student-teacher conference that helped Marisol clarify her purpose and plan additional strategies to substantiate her argument. We also worked on grammar, usage, and word choice.

Marisol's final draft (her sixth) appears as Appendix B and shows considerable expansion and improvement. She focuses on her thesis throughout, offering both specific and general examples to back up her assertions. The improvement in language and style is remarkable and might be written off as outside editing were it not for the evidence of later essay starts. These suggest that Marisol internalized many of the corrections she made on her drafts as she revised, even corrections that dropped out of this essay like her misspelling *refrigitator,* a form of which she later used correctly in a memorandum written for a different class (Appendix C). Her in-class final exam essay also showed significantly greater ease in writing in English. As part of her final portfolio evaluation, Marisol says the following of the animal intelligence essay: "I found it very hard to support the idea that humans have a higher capacity to learn than animals because I am an animal lover. However, I believe that I have supported the essay's thesis with enough examples, and I have made my point. Also, I included in the essay images and metaphors to attract my readers' attention."

About the overall portfolio, she says, "This portfolio clearly shows the improvement of my writing from early drafts to my final product. Also, this portfolio shows how dynamic my writing has become."

Again the revision process appears to lead this student to satisfaction. She claims each essay and the total portfolio as her own product; she recognizes her improvement and takes pride in her own authority.

Tangible evidence exists to show that what Marisol learned in one class carried over into others. This is apparent in a memorandum she wrote near the end of the same semester for a pre-engineering course. The memo reached me coincidentally because the engineering professor wanted me to see examples of successful freshman student writing in his field. He did not know that Marisol had studied writing in my class. The memo (included as Appendix C) shows evidence of continued second-language interference, but, when considered against her early unedited prose, indicates that Marisol has used techniques learned in one class to assist in the writing tasks of the other. She has focused, revised, and edited in her attempt to produce a successful paper. All indications are positive for continued success as Marisol enters her sophomore year.

Karen and Marisol were not the top students in their respective classes either at the beginning or at the end of the semester. They were both, however, extremely hard workers with a strong desire to succeed and, in this, not unusual among the students I have the privilege of meeting in my classes. While their final drafts indicate a need for further maturation and more writing practice, their growth offers evidence that it is possible to help students bridge the gap between expressive and academic writing through a gradual move from personal response to public writing *within a given essay.* The process must be taught; early drafts must be read with patience and optimism. Success comes slowly and only with considerable effort on the part of students and teachers, and teachers cannot assume that by the end of first-year composition all students will have mastered academic writing. Progress, while slow, becomes increasingly obvious as students discover the pleasure of self-improvement, willingly claim authority over their writing, and go on to be successful in other situations that require academic rhetoric.

NOTE

The concept of voice is in itself tricky and has been discussed elsewhere. See, for example, Laurie Finke's article "Feminism, Voice, and the Pedagogical Unconscious." *College English* 55(1) January 1993: 7–27. Finke calls "the metaphor of voice…an essential notion of a core 'self' who produces language or 'voice' manufactured out of 'experiences,…. Yet all of these terms—self, voice, experience—have been placed under erasure by poststructuralist semiotics and by Lacanian psychoanalysis" (13). Writers, then, do not find a voice so much as they create one out of their varied experiences, and both experience and voice remain open to multiple interpretations. Others who have written about voice include Patricia Bissell, Lisa Ede, Joseph Harris, Andrea Lundsford, and Louise Wetherbee Phelps.

WORKS CITED

Adler-Kassner, Linda. "Ownership Revisited." *College Composition and Communication*, 49(2), 208–33, May 1998.

Bartholomae, David. "Inventing the University." In Mike Rose (Ed.). *When a Writer Can't Write: Studies in Writer's Block and Other Composing Process Problems* (pp. 134–65). New York: Guilford, 1985.

Belenky, Mary Field, & Blythe McVicker Clinchy, Nancy Rule Goldberger, & Jill Mattuck Tarule. *Women's Ways of Knowing: The Development of Self, Voice, and Mind.* New York: Basic, 1986.

Bem, Sandra Lipsitz. *The Lenses of Gender: Transforming the Debate on Sexual Equality.* New Haven: Yale University Press, 1993.

Brannon, Lil & C.H. Knoblauch. "On Students' Rights to Their Own Texts." *College Composition and Communication*, 33, 157–66, 1982.

Carroll, Jeffrey. "Giving and Taking: A Note on Ownership." *The Writing Instructor*, 11(1), 17–21, Fall 1991.

Clark, Carol Lea and Students of English 1803. "Student Voices: How Students Define Themselves as Writers." In Sheryl L. Fontaine & Susan Hunter (Eds.). *Writing Ourselves Into the Story: Unheard Voices from Composition Studies* (pp. 215–28). Carbondale: Southern Illinois University, 1991.

Epstein, Cynthia Fuchs. *Deceptive Distinctions: Sex, Gender, and the Social Order.* New Haven: Yale University Press, 1988.

Flynn, Elizabeth. "Composition Studies from a Feminist Perspective." In Richard Bullock & John Trimbur (Eds.). *The Politics of Writing Instruction* (pp.137–54). Portsmouth, NH: Boynton/Cook, 1991.

Freire, Paulo. *Pedagogy of the Oppressed.* New York: Seabury, 1970.

Giroux, Henry A. *Schooling and the Struggle for Public Life: Critical Pedagogy in the Modern Age.* Minneapolis: University of Minnesota Press, 1988.

Giroux, Henry A. *Teachers as Intellectuals: Toward a Critical Pedagogy of Learning.* New York: Bergin & Garvey, 1988.

Harris, Muriel. *Teaching One-to-One: The Writing Conference.* Urbana, IL: NCTE, 1986.

Horner, Bruce. "Students, Authorship, and the Work of Composition." *College English*, 59.5, 505–529, September 1997.

Kirsch, Gesa. *Women Writing the Academy: Audience, Authority, and Transformation.* Carbondale: Southern Illinois University Press, 1993.

Knoblauch, C.H. & Lil Brannon (Eds.). *Rhetorical Traditions and the Teaching of Writing.* Upper Montclair, NJ: Boynton/Cook, 1984.

Lewis, Magda Gere. *Without a Word: Teaching Beyond Women's Silence.* New York: Routledge, 1993.

Maher, Frances A. "Toward a Richer Theory of Feminist Pedagogy: A comparison of 'liberation' and 'gender' models for teaching and learning." *Journal of Education*, 169.3, 91–100, 1987.

Miller, Richard, E. "The Nervous System." *College English*, 58 (3), 265–86, March 1996.

Penrose, Ann M. & Cheryl Geisler. "Reading and Writing Without Authority." *College Composition and Communication*, 45 (4), 505–20, December 1994.

Phelps, Louise Wetherbee. "Images of Student Writing: The Deep Structure of Teacher Response." In Chris Anson (Ed.). *Writing and Response: Theory, Practice, and Research.* Ed. Chris Anson. Urbana, IL: NCTE, 1989.

Ritchie, Joy S. "Resistance to Reading: Another View of the Minefield." *JAC: A Journal of Composition Theory*, 12.1, JAC Online, 1–17, 1992.

Schwegler, Robert A. "The Politics of Reading Student Papers." In Richard Bullock & John Trimbur (Eds.). *The Politics of Writing Instruction: Postsecondary.* Portsmouth, NH: Boynton/Cook, 1991.

Spigelman, Candace. "Habits of Mind: Historical Configurations of Textual Ownership in Peer Writing Groups." *College Composition and Communication*, 49 (2), 234–55, May 1998.

APPENDIX A: KAREN'S FINAL DRAFT
Poverty: Struggles of Children Below the Line

We Americans live in a nation where diversity is considered beneficial. Many problems, however, are caused by these very differences that make the United States a land of many divisions. One of the most noticeable separations in our society is between the income levels of families. As citizens of a country where everyone should have equal opportunities, the individuals who lie below the thin line separating high- and middle-income classes from poverty seem to be at a disadvantage in leading fulfilling lifestyles. Perhaps the most disturbing aspect of poverty is the effect that it has on children, the future of our country. Although our government provides help for these children, they undoubtedly encounter more obstacles than other children while growing up (Orcutt 16–18).

First, individuals below the poverty line cannot meet basic expenses. On a day-to-day basis, children need food, clothing, school supplies, and proper health care. If these needs are not satisfied because parents are unable to provide for them, children are at risk of being removed from their families and placed in foster care. They also may experience health problems more frequently than other children. Although chronic illness, childhood communicable diseases, infant mortality, depression, and hopelessness are a part of every socioeconomic class, it is becoming increasingly clear that these horrible situations exist mostly in the lower socioeconomic groups (Fitzgerald 9–10).

Being uprooted from a family can produce positive or negative effects on a child's development. Some children who live in poverty are raised by angry and frustrated parents who are unable to give enough attention to children due to their financial situations. Census data from 1990 indicates that almost twenty-five percent of the five million poor American children under the age of six lived with a single parent who worked full time. In cases like these, children can sometimes miss the proper maternal education and warmth needed to develop their cognitive intelligence, therefore making placement in other families the most logical thing to do. In other circumstances, when children are removed from loving, caring parents, there is often more harm done than good. These children may feel insecure, lonely, or scared, and may experience psychological problems throughout their lives (Fitzgerald xvi–xvii).

In addition to family life, poor children face problems in their environment as well. Many children living in poverty conditions have no other choice but to live in dangerous neighborhoods. If their parents are unable to afford moving to a better environment, children may be forced to live in the inner-city projects or neighborhoods for most of their childhood and adolescence. This makes them extremely susceptible to falling into the traps of gang participation and drug use. Even those children who put their guard up against drugs and gangs are still at higher risk of being injured or killed by gang activities than children from higher income families (Jarrett 30).

Finally, an important existing problem facing poor children is their need for acceptance by society. Today, many poor children attend the same schools as wealthy children, becoming aware of material possessions that they may possibly never have. In a world where being the best and having the most is considered ideal, less fortunate children may grow up feeling inferior to children who have more, although there is no significant difference between them as human beings. Other children may even shun or be judgmental of, the poor children because of the differences in their family lives.

Evidently, poverty is a major issue that upper- and middle-class America finds easiest to ignore. However, ignorance will not help the children who are suffering. According to 1990 census data, of all poor Americans, forty-two percent are black, thirty-five percent are Latino, thirty-four percent are Native American, and twenty-two percent are Asian American. By the end of the century, about thirty-eight and a half million United States citizens will live below poverty level, and by the year 2050, that number will approach approximately fifty million. Also, the United States had the highest rate of child poverty among the world's industrialized nations. These numbers can become dangerously high if the problem is left neglected.

Clearly, poverty is not entirely about race or culture. It is not about being the best or worst nation. It is not about percentages. Poverty is about people struggling to survive. We who are not victims of this problem can do our part by continuing to educate, care for, and communicate with those who suffer, instead of judging, shunning, and being too lazy ourselves to help them.

Works Consulted

America's Children. Washington: The National Council of Organizations for
     Children and Youth, 1976.
Fitzgerald, Hiram E. *Children of Poverty: Research, Health, and Policy
     Issues*. New York: Garland Publishing, Inc., 1995.
Jarrett, Robin L. "Living Poor: Family Life Among Single Parent, African
     American Women." *Social Problems*. Ed. Robert Perucci. Volume 41:

No. 1: February 1994. Berkley: University of California Press, 1994. 30–45.

Orcutt, Ben A. *Poverty and Social Casework Services.* Metuchen: The Scarecrow Press, Inc., 1974.

APPENDIX B: MARISOL'S FINAL DRAFT
Animals' Intelligence: Are Theirs Like Humans'?

There is no doubt in my mind that some animals can feel anger, love, sadness, happiness, and fear and that they have enough intelligence to learn new things. Animals, such as chimpanzees and dogs, have special learning abilities; however, animal intelligence will never be like humans' intelligence.

Dogs, for instance, are known as man's best friend because of their ability to fulfill almost every owner's needs. A good example of this is my seven-week-old puppy named Toby. He is a beige Chow-chow puppy, hyper enough to destroy an entire city. He likes to bite everything, except his new chewing toy, of course, and to feel how his jaws convert things into pieces. Also, it seems as if he enjoys waking me up at night. He wakes up around 4:00 A.M., and he does not stop playing until my alarm clock rings. There has not been a night that Toby has not growled, cried, and/or barked as if inviting me to his private party under the stars.

Toby's lively and bright personality has always been in him; however, he is starting to learn how to control it. Now, the puppy seems to understand when someone corrects him or praises him. When he hears a strong, sharp voice calling at him, he hides his tail between his legs and lowers his ears. On the other hand, the puppy's whole body shakes with excitement when I pronounce "Toby" in a soft voice.

Toby's intelligence is obvious. Hopefully, he will learn to stay, sit, roll down, pick up the newspaper, guard the house, bring me my sleepers, and, most important, not to bark at night. Almost every dog owner will agree with me that dogs can learn, with a little bit of effort, everything mentioned.

Who does not remember Lassie, Benji, Rintintin, or Beethoven? These dogs have shown their ability to learn in movies and TV series. This Collie, Terrier, German Shepher, and Saint Bernard were trained to be stars. I remember a scene in one of Benji's movies where he is forced to take care of four baby tigers. After the baby's mother is killed, Benji tries to find them a stepmother. Through their journey, one tiger falls into a river. Benji, knowing the tiger is too little to fight the river's current, jumps to his rescue. He grabs the baby's neck, swims to the river's bank, and saves the tiger's life. Benji was outstanding; his intelligence surpassed other animal's intelligence. However, can we expect a dog to be able to add, make tools, talk, or communicate through American Sign Language? Of course not. Benji did not know how to act or how to perform tricks; he learned them. Moreover, it does not matter how many years I spend trying to teach Toby ASL, he will not learn it. It is clear dogs have special talents; however, they are limited.

Chimpanzees are very similar to dogs. They also have the ability to learn and to express what they feel, but their abilities go further. A great example is in Jane goodal's story from "The Mind of the Champanzee." In this story, Goodal mentions how Lucy, an eight-year-old chimpanzee, learned to communicate through American Sign Language. Thanks to this language, Lucy was able to express her thoughts. If she wanted something, she made the hand movement necessary to express, "This is Lucys."

The extraordinary learning ability chimpanzees have does not end with Lucy's example. Washoe is a highly intelligent chimpanzee, also mentioned in Goodal's story, who takes Lucy's accomplishment one step further. Washoe did not only learn the ASL signs, but also taught them to her little chimpanzee pupil, Loulis. It is important to mention that even Washoe taught Loulis the ASL signs correctly. Louis either misspelled the words and/or he did not learn them at all.

Chimpanzees' broader intelligence exceeds dogs', not only because they can express their feelings in a more human way, but also because they have many biological and physical humanlike characteristics. For example, chimpanzees, like humans, have special fingers called thumbs that allow them to grab things and do things such as write, paint, open a door, grab a glass of mile, and/or eat with a spoon. Also, chimpanzees' DNA is so close to humans that they can get sick with diseases associated only for humans, such as AIDS or hepatitis B. Moreover, humans' and chimpanzees' organs are so similar that surgeons have made human transplants using chimpanzees' organs. All these similarities show how close, but not equal, chimps are to humans.

What is then the difference between animals' and humans' intelligence? In Toby's case, learning was encouraged in part by memories of continuous situations. What I mean is that every time Toby did something wrong, I called to him with a strong voice and scolded him with a little slap. Also, when I played with him, I used a soft voice and/or gave him a treat. I understand that he has also learned some things on his own, like eating or cleaning himself, but that is called a survival instinct—if he does not eat, he dies. Toby has learned by repetition, instinct, survival, scoldings or rewards. It is not as if the puppy wakes one morning and decides to learn a new trick.

Also, Benji's intelligent acts were influenced by humans. The movie director and Benji's trainer taught him what to do and when to do it.

Chimpanzee learning, on the other hand, is encouraged by either humans or other animals. For instance, a chimpanzee in his/her natural habitat would never learn the ASL signs without human intervention. Even though a trained chimpanzee is deliberately left in the jungle to teach other chimps, the learning chain will not go very far. For example, in Washoe's case, Loulis did not learn the language correctly and, sometimes, he even made up words. If two chimpanzees were not able to learn exactly the same language, how can we expect a thousand to do it?

Many people may argue that chimps have developed a way of communication (through sounds, gestures, groans, and movements), so they do not differ many from us. Nevertheless, this system is not precise and may lead to confusion. For instance, when two male chimpanzees fight for power or territory, almost every chimpanzee near starts barking, yelling, growling, and/or making all kind of noises. Some of them may bark because they are afraid, some others because they disagree with the fight, or even some may yell as they support one opponent. In other words, chimpanzees' sounds are indescriminate.

It is important to mention that even though chimpanzees are physically and biologically adapted to live as human beings, they do not use all their capacity. For example, chimpanzees vocal cords are so like humans' that chimps could talk; however they do not use them for this purpose. Many paleontologists and anthropologists have tried to teach chimps a spoken language without success. It is obvious that chimpanzees also have a limitation that does not allow them to have a human life.

There is no doubt that chimpanzees are intelligent, that they communicate and teach. However, their learning abilities are limited. They do not have the necessity of knowledge humans have. Humans have always wondered about how things work, why do they work, why a day is cold or hot, how the clouds form, what makes us sick, what happen inside our bodies, and/or what makes a tree grow. Humans like to know, and they are not satisfied with knowing facts, but they like to find a scientific explanation for everything. Humans' curiosity has led them to wonder about diseases and cures. For example, when the first cases of AIDS were reported, scientists did not know how the patients got the disease, or if it was contagious or not. After many years of hard working, scientists discovered the HIV virus, which caused AIDS, and they found out that this virus was either transmitted through sexual intercourse or through the use of infected needles. However, humans have not surrender to the fight against AIDS. Now, scientists want to know more about it, and they are desperately looking for a cure of this infectious disease that affects 6000 people per day.

Moreover, humans' intelligence exceeds animals' because humans think, analyze, and choose the best answer to a problem. For instance, on a cloudy morning, it is common to see a man taking his jacket, umbrella, and coffee in hand when leaving his house. He knows that without his coat and umbrella, he may get wet., which may get him a cold. He undestands the consequences of his acts, analyzes, and chooses. That is why the scientific name for humans comes from the Latin words *Homo Sapiens* that mean *Thinking Human.*

Humans, as we can see, exceed chimpanzees' and dogs' intelligence by having a higher capacity to learn and to apply what they have learned. By saying this, I am not trying to start a human superiority campaign, but to show the different levels of learning capacities between species. There is no doubt that intelligence can be found not only in humans, but also in animals; the only difference is that nature has distributed it in different degrees between the creatures of this planet.

APPENDIX C: Marisol's Memorandum

TO: The Honorable Gonzalo Barrientos
                US Senator
FROM: Marisol A........., technical consultant trainee
DATE: April 7, 1997
SUBJECT: Should the production of freon (dichlorodifluoromethane) be banned?

In response to your request for background information on ozone depletion by CFMs or dichlorodifluoromethanes, I am providing a short scientific description of CFMs' chemic reaction in the atmosphere. Also, I inform you of the economical impact consumers have suffered since freon has been banned, as well as a recommendation of either or not sponsor a repeal to freon's ban in the US. I can provide more detailed information if it is needed.

Ozone molecules are form when the action of ultraviolet radiation acts on $O2$ of oxygen molecules. An accumulation of ozone molecules in the stratosphere (between altitudes of 10 to 15 km) is usually referred to as the *ozone layer.* It is important to mention that ozone molecules are unstable and can be created and destroyed continuously by chemical reaction between gases in the stratosphere. The ozone-destroying reaction involve atomic oxygen, atomic chloride, or oxides of elements such as hydrogen, nitrogen, and chloriene (which is a CFM component).

According to M.J. Molina and F.S. Rowland, CFMs are a threat of the ozone layer because these gases are long-lived gases that break down only in the stratosphere and release their chlorine there. Chain reaction produced by chlorine atoms and CIO deplete the ozone layer. CFMs' dangerous impact in the ozone layer is also supported by the Committe on Impacts of Stratospheric Change in its report *Environmental Effects on Chlorodifluromethane Release* (1976). This report predicted an ozone reduction of 0.5% or the amount of that year's CFMs release was maintained.

Moreover, soon after the Antarctic ozone hole was discover, an open scientific debate was raised, as well as numerous experiments. For example in 1986 a novel mechanism converted inactive chlorine such as HCl into reactive ozone-destroying forms such as CLO. The patterns released by this experiment were later measured inside the Antarctic ozone hole. The experiment's results gave the scientific community enough evidence to think that the primary cause of depletion was the increase of CFCs and related halocarbons as CFMs.

This evidence and scientific support justified freon's ban in the US. It is important to mention that not only the United States have banned the production of freon, but also numerous countries including Canada, Sweden, Norway, The United Kingdom, Denmark, The Russian Federation, Italy, France, Brazil.

Unfortunately, this ban has provoke an economic struggle within freon's consumers. For example, General Motors has used freon as refrigerant for decades. Without freon GM would have to spend billions of dollars trying to redesign the entire refrigeration systems in home, industrial, and commercial equipment. Replacing just the refrigerated transport of food would cost over 150 billion dollars. Also, the cost of converting a car's air conditioning system varies from $180 to $250. In conclusion, estimates have put the cost of banning CFC's refrigerants at $800 per person, per year.

As you can see, the banning of freon has economically affected many Americans; however, a bigger cost we would have to pay if the ozone layer is destroyed. Besides, according to M. Prathener and F.S. Rouland the levels of cholorine loading expected under the Copenhagen '92 scenario (which suggested the CFC's shut down after 2002), and the ones actually recorded show a considerable difference. For example, if freon had been regulated until 2002 by 1990 a 9 p.p.b. chlorine concentration would have been in the atmosphere instead of the actual 4 p.p.b. Also, a 10% of ozone depletion would exceed by 2000 instead of just reaching 4% by 1997.

For the evidence mention above I recommend you not to support the repeal of freon's ban. Please do not hesitate to contact me if you have any question.

APPENDIX D: Guidelines for Evaluating Individual Essays

These guidelines are designed for the purpose of self-evaluation.[1] They will help those students who find deferred grading disconcerting because, at any time, you can evaluate your own work on the basis of these criteria. You may also ask fellow writers to rate your work by using these guidelines. At the end of the semester, you will use this rubric to assist your instructor in deciding your final grade for the class.

Purpose
A   Establishes and maintains a clear purpose and focus.
B   Establishes a purpose and focus.
C   Attempts to establish a purpose; focus of writing not fully clear.
D   Purpose and focus not apparent.

Organization
A   Organized from beginning to end. Logical progression of ideas. Fluent and coherent.
B   Organization moves paper forward with few lapses in unity and coherence.
C   Lapse(s) in organization affect unity and coherence.
D   Serious errors in organization make writing difficult to follow.

Details
A   Details are pertinent, vivid, or explicit and provide ideas/information in depth.
B   Details develop ideas/information *or* details are elaborated.
C   Details lack elaboration, merely listed, or unnecessarily repetitious.
D   Details are minimal, inappropriate, random, or perfunctory.

Voice or Tone
A   Distinctive personal expression or distinctive tone enhances writing.
B   Establishes personal expression/effective tone.
C   Attempts personal expression/appropriate tone.
D   Personal expression/appropriate tone not evident.

Grammar/Usage/Mechanics
A   Few or no errors present *or* departures from convention intentional and effective.
B   Some errors or patterns of errors are present.
C   Numerous errors are likely to distract reader.
D   Errors omnipresent and/or interfere with understanding.

NOTE

These guidelines are adapted from an NCTE Council Chronicle.

CHAPTER SIX
Risktakers: Developing a Playful Attitude Toward Writing

Until the 1960s, secondary and higher education in the United States was geared toward traditional-aged (18–24), middle-class students. Everyone recognized that other kinds of students attended classes, but these others did not serve as an educational model. Instruction centered around what teachers did, and activities, more often than not, focused on responses from white male students. In the 1960s, an influx of returning veterans necessitated more open admission policies for postsecondary education. At the same time, women began agitating strenuously for equal opportunities, and other minority groups became vocal about demanding their civil rights.

This combination of forces led to a new educational paradigm that included student-centered instruction and a more inclusive attitude toward nonmainstream students. Teachers and administrators began to consider "the whole child," and curriculum expanded with the addition of special-interest courses and a wide array of extracurricular activities that made up a regular part of the school week. Interest grew in learning communities and classroom games. While some of these innovations became accepted as the norm, interest in building community and in teaching through play waned over the next decades. Today, educators and the general public often dismiss play activities as inappropriate for school. This is a serious mistake because games and simulations can serve a valuable educational function, not only for children, but also for adults. They have special appeal for nontraditional learners who may have trouble meshing with mainstream students or who feel incapable of success due to language barriers, physical disabilities, or other problems that make them feel like outsiders. A playful classroom atmosphere makes all students feel welcome, and games can draw class members together, ease fears, and encourage risk-taking.

A Definition of Play

Based on his notions of reversal theory and his belief in the importance of "frequent changes or reversals in mental states" (13–29), Michael Apter defines play as "a state of mind, a way of seeing and being, a special mental 'set' towards the world and one's actions in it" (13). He says that games provide a "protective frame" that lets players forget fears of inadequacy and enjoy themselves as they participate. Lenore Terr makes a clear distinction between leisure, which is passive, and play, which is active. She calls play "an activity directed primarily at having fun" (28) and notes that it usually follows a particular format and has time limits and rules. She also equates play with attitude: "We know we are playing when we are suddenly removed from cares and worries. We know because afterward we feel cleansed and refreshed" (28).

Educators do not want school to be perceived as leisure time, but they do encourage active learning that makes students feel relaxed and satisfied. Thus they might choose to define play in its broadest sense, referring more to the participants' attitudes toward an activity than to the nature of the activity itself. By this definition, any activity undertaken in a spirit of playfulness becomes play. This explains Tom Sawyer's success in finding helpers to whitewash Aunt Polly's fence. Samuel Clemens knew that boys (real and fictional) who might shun an activity they considered "work" would happily engage in the same activity if they perceived it as "fun." In fact, play pervades every aspect of human function. Jean Piaget says, "practically every form of psychological activity is initially enacted in play" (in Wilson, 9). Play aids cognitive development. The baby playing peek-a-boo learns eventually that closing her eyes does not make others disappear; youngsters sifting sand at the beach learn the laws of conservation; playing house teaches role differentiation; playing football teaches elements of geometry and physics. Play also encourages language acquisition and fluency through nursery rhymes, tongue twisters, puns, riddles, and similar activities. Although generalized play may have no specific, articulated purpose, classroom games always have a recognized goal. The teacher may or may not announce the goal to students, but she must know the purpose and expected outcomes of each activity.

Theory of Play

One of the first theorists to support educational play, Johan Huizinga wrote in the 1930s about the value of play as a way to preserve culture, and William Stephenson, writing in 1988, warns about the dangers of categorizing activities like work and play instead of weaving them together. Stephenson suggests that play adds "a leavening of enjoyment" (60) to serious activities and that in an ideal world, work should be fun.

Cultural theorists (Cole, 1985, 1990, 1996; Forman et al., 1993; Guzzetti & Hynd, 1998; McGilly, 1994; Rogoff, 1990; Sutton-Smith, 1997) continue to support Huizinga's notions. They believe that students learn through social contexts in the classroom contexts that actively engage them in creating knowledge. Because games are, by their very nature, dynamic, they place students in situations where they must work with classmates to come up with new ideas and imagine solutions to ever-changing problems. As new situations present themselves in the context of the game, players need to adapt, to consult with fellow players, to form opinions, make guesses, and take risks. Thus they learn by doing rather than by being told what to do, and, as a bonus, they bond with their teammates and learn important lessons about collaboration. Sutton-Smith claims that play also helps students by replicating the real world. Successful game players feel more powerful in class and, consequently, in the world.

Lev Vygotsky (1926), pioneer in educational psychology, believed that learning through personal experience carried more weight than narratives of the experiences of others. He felt well-planned games could "organize the higher form of behavior, involve the resolution of rather complex problems of behavior, require guess-work, quickness, and resourcefulness, and the concerted and coordinated efforts of the most diverse capacities and forces" (90). According to Vygotsky, "Psychology requires that students learn not only to perceive, but also to respond" (48). Classroom games create both desire and urgency for response.

Women, members of ethnic minorities, people with disabilities, and other nontraditional students profit most from play that is cooperative rather than competitive. According to learning community theorists (Baloche, 1998; Johnson & Johnson, 1988; et al., 1983; Schmuck & Schmuck, 1997; Slavin, 1990) noncompetitive games reduce learner anxiety and classroom hierarchies while also helping people of different backgrounds and abilities accept one another as equals.

Barbara Rogoff also recognizes the value of learning communities and articulates links between collaborative and cultural theory. She encourages situations where learners collaborate with more skilled participants, creating what Vygotsky called a "zone of proximal development." In this "zone," learners can tackle problems slightly beyond their present competence level because they are assisted by others who know more than they do. Thus, they face continual challenges without fear of failure, confident that they can rely on the expertise of more experienced cohorts. Educators who worry that play will disrupt classroom decorum can find assurance of its educational value by studying what theorists have to say.

Classroom Play

Critics of classroom play argue that teachers should educate, not amuse or entertain, their students. Certainly they are correct, but games do not merely entertain; they attract students to tasks they might otherwise fear or reject and engage them in activities that lead, often without their awareness, to learning. Conrad Hyers says the goal of educational play "is not to achieve a momentary fever pitch of excitement, but to cultivate inquisitiveness and fascination. Education is not a kind of show business juggling, but a juggling with ideas and possibilities" (138). Young people (and many fortunate older people) have a natural spirit of fun that teachers often look at as naughtiness that needs to be squelched. In fact, that spirit has enormous pedagogical potential that teachers can harness and use in their own best interests and those of their students. Through games and simulations, they can encourage students who think poetry is "silly stuff" to write song lyrics. They can offer teens who "hate Shakespeare" opportunities to write and perform modern-day versions of the classic plays. They can play punctuation Bingo with young people who think they are "turned off" by language rules. Secondary school students love these kinds of activities, and, surprisingly, so do adults. Terr laments the loss of occasions to play as people reach adolescence and touts the benefits of play for all ages. "Play makes people scintillate," she says. "It creates a kind of mental click that frees you to begin sorting things out.... It may well be that an overall lack of play dulls society" (20). A valuable but unexpected outcome of classroom play may be teachers rediscovering their own playfulness as they serve as facilitator and audience to their students' unleashed creativity. The end result can be a classroom where all members enjoy themselves as they learn together.

Some teachers, parents, and administrators fail to see this potential, especially when students' success is judged mainly by performance on standardized tests. However, according to Vygotsky, play is never frivolous because people are playful beings whose "games always have a larger meaning" (89). With careful planning, execution, and follow-up, classroom games can help students develop skills, including those they need to be successful on tests. Gaming provides what Rogoff has called "an apprenticeship in learning"; she encourages the presentation of new situations and unfamiliar problems to novices who are helped to solutions by more skilled partners. This is the way games work. Playing in teams, classmates figure out answers together, depending on each other as they reach beyond what they are sure of. Competitive games can also serve a purpose. Teachers can take potential test items and turn them into classroom Jeopardy or Concentration games. By adding a timer, they can help students get used to giving answers quickly. Played with gusto because they are perceived as games, students get practice from activities that may help raise their test scores.

Writing and Play

A major problem for nontraditional students is fear of failure. They feel especially fearful when they face a writing task because writing tends to reveal the writer's feelings and flaws. Sometimes they bring with them previous experiences of failure. Many students may perceive themselves as "different" or "unacceptable." If they are in any way different from the majority of class members—or even if they are like class members but different from the teacher—they may feel they do not belong or do not "fit." They worry that they will not be able to measure up. Games can provide a powerful release from this type of anxiety. When they are presented in the right spirit, students come to see games as worry-free time where wrong answers are ignored in a team's effort to find consensus about the best possible choice. Writing done as part of a game or simulation does not "count"; grades are not recorded. Losing a game does not matter because, after all, it is only a game. Paul Chance sees freedom to fail as one of the best justifications for classroom play. He says this freedom allows learners a chance to "explore the outer limits" of their skills, "thereby extending those limits" (22). Teachers can present students with very difficult problems or writing tasks, call finding the answers or finishing the piece a game, and watch students work happily on what would otherwise have frightened or intimidated them.

Classroom Simulations

Apter says that games provide a "protective frame" that shields players from reality, thus making them feel secure and unthreatened (15). This means they are free to be creative, to try methods they have not tried before, and to approach questions from new angles. Alice Gordon suggests that the best games provide an "opportunity to deal with complex problems in extremely concrete ways" (16). Just as the game of Chess finds its origins in war strategy, educational games aim to teach important concepts. A magazine simulation should teach students about audience, research, and style while at the same time giving young writers a venue for creativity and self-expression. The outcomes of classroom play must be greater than having fun, or winning, or even developing an impressive product (like a finished class magazine). Students should also come away from the experience with usable skills and understandings about the subject matter of the class and about society in general.

Many of these skills and awarenesses come about as the result of cooperation. John Hollowell and Kenneth Davis suggest that playing games in class helps move away from teacher control to student-centered learning because "games stimulate student involvement in solving a new problem, mastering new skills, or practicing old skills in new contexts" (3). These authors also point out the highly motivational aspect of play and the opportunities it offers for immediate feedback. As students work together toward common goals, they must necessarily communicate, thus improving verbal and interpersonal skills. They learn to accept criticism and make changes as they work based on the opinions of their peers. As they get help with grammar from one classmate and creative suggestions regarding content from another, they also discover that individuals make different kinds of contributions, so they come to value diversity.

Simulations generally do not include competition and, therefore, make excellent learning games. A simulation involves setting up a situation modeled on actual life experience where students assume roles and perform designated tasks. Roles and tasks are assigned by choice or by selecting game cards. A restaurant simulation might include the roles of menu writer, newspaper food critic, advertisement copywriter, and health inspector. Cards would include roles and duties of each (writing a menu with vivid descriptions of each offering, writing a critique of a meal chosen from the menu, providing the original recipe for a French dish with an English translation, etc.). Each team member produces an individual piece using resources like cookbooks, newspapers, and trade publications, then submits them to the group for peer review. After revision, the finished packet is submitted and shared with the entire class. Some teachers give group or individual grades for specified parts of the simulation, but the activities may be so motivating that grades are not necessary at all.

In a marketplace simulation, one group of students may work together to create a used-book store. Some members will concern themselves with soliciting donations through team-written appeal letters, while others will produce advertisements, or write book summaries or author biographies. Group members may decide to offer foreign language books as part of their store, thus necessitating a student to organize, advertise, and sell to speakers of Korean, or Spanish, or Chinese. Such activity allows each student to shine, even those who have previously felt unsuccessful in the classroom. It also integrates skills from various classes and makes learning more relevant and less fragmented than it might be in situations where each class remains separate.

Possible simulations are only limited by the imaginations of teachers and students. They can be developed around newspaper or magazine publication, criminal investigation, court cases, sports events, politics, specific literary works, or any number of topics. They may also be developed in response to current events. One simulation I have observed personally involves the use of erector sets in a technical writing class. Groups build a product using their erector set and then write reports, marketing brochures, and other materials related to their particular product. Students can even invent and produce their own simulations. Obviously simulations should be geared to the grade level, subject, and interests of a given audience with tasks appropriate to the desired learning outcomes.

Nonsimulation Games

A disadvantage to simulations is that they require extended periods of time—often weeks, months, or even entire semesters. Not all settings allow for this type of activity, but other kinds of games can be played in periods as short as fifteen minutes and still provide the advantages of cooperative play. Any game played as a team encourages shared knowledge, negotiation, and collaboration. One very popular writing game places teams of students (or individuals) in competition with the teacher. "Stump the Teacher" requires an overhead projector and student access to transparencies. The individual or team takes a passage from a literary work and types it onto a transparency along with an original passage aimed to imitate the style of the author. The teacher then projects the samples and must decide which of the two is the original. The teacher gets a point for a correct answer. The team gets points for a miss. Students learn about sentence structure, word choice, diction, and other elements of style as they play this game. When played regularly at intervals, their skills improve remarkably as the challenge grows to outwit the teacher. This game also serves the purpose of empowering students and making them feel close to the teacher who is willing to take part in their games and cede points to them while acknowledging their clever use of language.

Competition presented as play may also help students learn. Whereas students may feel insecure and unhappy in a test situation, they may willingly play a game like "Classroom Concentration." For this game, the teacher (or student helpers) creates a large chart of covered squares. Under each flap is the name of an author or literary work or quotation. Students take turns attempting to match the author with either a title or a quotation. They score points for correct matches. This activity may be conducted in a team setting or individuals may compete. Obviously, this is extremely adaptable and could be used for memorizing states and their capitals, books and publication dates, or any similar matching tasks. Promising students that they can play "Classroom Concentration" often stimulates them to study material they would otherwise find dull.

Rules of Play

Game playing requires rules and generally takes place within a specified time frame. According to Huizinga, play is characterized by its extraordinary nature; that is, play differs from "real" life. This element of unreality is what makes students feel free to take risks. Still, it must have structure, purpose, and rules that allow it to proceed "within its own proper boundaries of time and space according to fixed rules and in an orderly manner" (Huizinga, 13). Rules of play may be practiced first in short activities. "Simon Says," a game already familiar to most students and easily adaptable to most subject areas, can serve as an example. A language arts teacher can gear it toward vocabulary review by issuing instructions to students such as, "Simon says, 'Inscribe your signature on the chalkboard' " or "Simon says, 'Acknowledge an acquaintance's accomplishments.' " Even simple games like this must be run according to a set of regulations. Thirty middle-schoolers hurrying to write their names on the chalkboard can create pandemonium unless they proceed quietly without pushing or other disturbances. Obviously they must understand that games will not continue if they disturb surrounding classes or if confusion reigns.

One essential tool is a call to order. Many teachers use hand signals for this purpose. When the teacher raises her hand, students who see her immediately raise their own hands and become quiet. This has a domino effect, which silences the class in a matter of seconds. It also impresses any unexpected visitor. Some teachers flash the lights instead of raising a hand; others use a bell. The method matters less than frequent practice. In most classes, the quieting mechanism becomes its own game, and students try to beat their own record for achieving silence.

Interactive activities can teach students lessons in propriety and levels of language. Students like to play the game where they take turns adding to a team story. One student writes a paragraph and passes the story to the next student who adds the next paragraph. Obviously some students will be tempted to make silly or inappropriate additions that can damage the outcome. With the promise of play, teachers can discuss language levels, appropriate subject matter, colloquialism, slang, and jargon. They can explain how tone is established and ask students to use moderate or formal language and tone. If these rules are breached, the team's entry is removed from competition. This lesson also works when students play the sentence game. In this activity, the teacher asks one player from each team to write an independent clause. Player two must add a prepositional phrase. Player three adds a dependent clause, and so forth. Students playing these games learn about language as they also discover that writing can be fun.

Games with equipment need rapid assembly and cleanup. Class members can select role cards for setting up and putting away materials or each member can accept a portion of this duty on a regular basis. It works well, for example, if each group member brings his or her chair along as groups form and also takes responsibility for returning it to its proper place after the activity. This is particularly important when teachers travel from one class to another and are followed by other classes, as is the case in most colleges and universities. (Yes, games work at this level and are appreciated as long as they have a clearly apparent purpose.) Of course, someone needs to keep track of time and allow for cleanup. The teacher can do this, or an alternating timekeeper can be selected.

Establishing time guidelines gives organized play a finite quality and prevents it from dying out with a whimper. Short games played at the end of class have a natural termination point with the ringing of a bell. These contrast sharply with long-term activities like simulations that may continue for weeks or months.

The Importance of Risk

Educators may assume that students come to school willingly, eager to learn and comfortable with their peers, but this assumption is not true for all students. Nontraditional learners often enter the classroom filled with apprehension. They fear they will not live up to teacher or parent expectations. They worry that they will appear stupid and make mistakes that cause others to laugh at them. Even adults have similar fears, like the middle-aged African American woman returning to school and finding herself in a classroom full of bright-eyed white teenagers. "I can't even climb the stairs without panting," she complains. "How can I possibly keep up with them intellectually?"

Games provide ways to relieve fear and enable students to learn. Because teamwork and spontaneity characterize games, and because a playful atmosphere makes all students feel comfortable, educational play can help class members take chances they would otherwise avoid. This is especially important in writing classes where fear of failure can create writer's block or result in a stilted, unimaginative product. By contrast, when students feel motivated to write by the requirements of a game or simulation, they write more quickly and freely. They focus on the game's goal rather than a grade based on standards someone else has set—usually someone who represents traditional authority and not their own nontraditional reality.

Writing is hard work, but it does not deserve to be met with trepidation. Rather it should bring out a student's creativity and self-expression. Risk-taking student writers produce more volume, and they edit and revise more enthusiastically. Teachers should encourage this kind of behavior; games can help them achieve their purpose.

WORKS CITED

Apter, Michael J. "A Structural-Phenomenology of Play." In Kerr and Apter, 13–29.

Baloche, Lynda A. *The Cooperative Classroom: Empowering Learning.* Upper Saddle River, NJ: Prentice Hall, 1998.

Chance, Paul. *Learning Through Play.* New York: Gardner Press, 1979.

Cole, Michael. "The Zone of Proximal Development: Where Culture and Cognition Create Each Other." In J.V. Wertsch (Ed.). *Culture, Communication, and Cognition: Vygotskian Perspectives.* Cambridge: Cambridge University Press, 1985.

———. "Cognitive Development and Formal Schooling: The Evidence from Cross-cultural Research." In L. Moll (Ed.). *Vygotsky and Education: Instructional Implications and Applications of Sociohistorical Psychology* (pp. 89–110). Cambridge: Cambridge University Press, 1990.

———. *Cultural Psychology: A Once and Future Discipline.* Cambridge, MA: Harvard University Press. 1996.

Forman, E, N. Minick & C. Addison Stone. *Contexts for Learning: Sociocultural Dynamics in Children's Development.* New York: Oxford University Press, 1993.

Gordon, Alice Kaplan. *Games for Growth: Educational Games in the Classroom.* Chicago: Science Research Associates, 1972.

Guzzetti, Barbara, & Cynthia Hynd. *Perspectives on Conceptual Change: Multiple Ways to Understand Knowing and Learning in a Complex World.* Mahwah, NJ: Lawrence Erlbaum, 1998.

Hollowell, John & Kenneth Davis. *Inventing and Playing Games in the English Classroom: A Handbook for Teachers,* 1997.

Huizinga, Johan. *Homo Ludens: A Study of the Play-element in Culture.* Boston: Beacon Press, 1950.

Hyers, Conrad. "Education as Play." In Kerr and Apter. 13–29.

Johnson, David W. & R. T. Johnson. *Cooperation and Competition Theory and Research.* Englewood Cliffs, NJ: Lawrence Erlbaum, 1988.

Johnson, David W., R. T. Johnson, & G. Maruyama. "Interdependence and Interpersonal Attraction Among Heterogeneous and Homogeneous Individuals: A Theoretical Formulation and a Meta-analysis of the Research." *Review of Educational Research,* 53, 5–54, 1983.

Kerr, John A. & Michael J. Apter (Eds.). *Adult Play: A Reversal Theory Approach.* Amsterdam: Swets & Zeitlinger, 1990.

Lyman, L. & H. C. Goyle. *Cooperative Prouping for Interactive Learning: Students, Teachers and Administrators.* Washington, DC: National Education Association, 1990.

McGilly, K. *Classroom Lessons: Integrating Cognitive Theory and Classroom Practice.* Cambridge, MA: MIT Press, 1994.

Rogoff, Barbara. *Apprenticeship in Thinking: Cognitive Development in Social Context.* New York: Oxford University Press, 1990.

Schmuck, Richard A. & P. A. Schmuck. *Group Processes in the Classroom.* Seventh edition. Boston: McGraw-Hill, 1997.

Slavin, Robert *Cooperative Learning: Theory, Research, and Practice.* Englewood Cliffs, NJ: Prentice Hall, 1990.

Stephenson, William. *The Play Theory of Mass Communication.* New Brunswick and Oxford: Transaction Basics, 1988.

Sutton-Smith, Bryan. *The Ambiguity of Play.* Cambridge, MA: Harvard University Press, 1997.

Terr, Lenore. *Beyond Love and Work: Why Adults Need to Play.* New York: Scribner, 1999.

Vygotsky, Lev S. *Educational Psychology* Boca Raton, FL: St. Lucie Press, 1997 (Published originally in 1926, in Russian).

Wilson, R. Rawdon. *In Palamedes' Shadow: Explorations in Play, Game, and Narrative Theory.* Boston: Northeastern University Press, 1990.

CHAPTER SEVEN
Achievers: Writing Beyond (Dis)Ability

Perhaps the most challenging group of nontraditional students entering classrooms in recent decades are those who have been variously categorized as disabled, impaired, or special-needs students. Once a small minority, a recent estimate now labels 56 million Americans as people with disabilities (Brueggemann et al., 369), many of whom are school age. Often "passing" as able-bodied, these students confound educators because their impairments vary so widely and have such diverse consequences. Furthermore, most teachers have no training in recognizing or teaching this particular audience.

In the past two years alone, I have met students in my classes with identified visual, auditory, and learning impairments. Another of my students obviously had difficulty seeing, but refused to acknowledge the problem or accept accommodation. Surely classroom members also included others with undiagnosed or unacknowledged impairments such as dyslexia, Attention Deficit Disorder (ADD), hyperactivity, mental illness, diabetes, or any number of conditions that can inhibit classroom success. Like most teachers, I have had no training in recognizing these conditions or in teaching writing to students affected by them. Until this year, I had not read a single article on disability or discussed the issue with colleagues.

I am sure I would have continued in my ignorance had not a series of events shaken me out of my lethargy. First was an influx of students asking for accommodation. Second was my decision to write this book about non-traditional students in writing classrooms. Third, and perhaps most important to me personally, was my own rapidly diminishing eyesight. As my impairment increased and created more difficulties in my work and my life, I became more aware of the possible problems my students might be experiencing. In response to this combination of occurrences, I began reading about impaired students and about how the educational system unintentionally—indeed unknowingly—turns their impairment into disability. This chapter is my call for further research on teaching writing to students with varying degrees of impairment. No single methodology will suffice for all types or all degrees of impairment; rather, I hope that many educators will contribute what they have discovered about enabling students to write beyond (dis)ability.

Choosing the Right Words

When I first became interested in the question of impairment, I realized that I did not know how to talk about it. Like most people, I feared that I might use the wrong terminology and inadvertently insult someone. Clearly, no productive discussion can take place without a usable vocabulary, so I began searching for the right words. My search led to more questions. I discovered that the language used to discuss disability has undergone considerable change in recent decades, but vocabulary still remains controversial. The terms *handicapped, retarded, blind, deaf* have, in many situations, given way to the less specific *disabled* or *impaired*. In other instances, however, even more specific terms are preferred (autistic, hyperactive, dyslexic, etc.). Dr. Martin Sullivan recommends using the guidelines established by the Union of the Physically Impaired Against Segregation (UPIAS) in 1975. According to these guidelines, "*impairment* means a wide range of defective physical, sensory, cognitive and psychological mechanisms of the body or mind and *disability* is the disadvantage caused by the social, economic, political and environmental factors which restrict and/or exclude people with impairment from full participation in their communities" (2). Sullivan feels we should follow the social rather than the medical model of disability because it identifies society rather than the impaired individual as the disabling agent. This seems to me a productive way for teachers to approach students with special needs. Just as a student from another country needs specific kinds of lessons that take language interference into account, so does a student with a learning disability or reduced vision need accommodation. Students are not at fault if their first language is French, nor should they take any blame for a physical or mental impairment. The problem for teachers is clearly social rather than medical. A student using a wheelchair does not represent a medical emergency. She enters the class as a learner. Perhaps she cannot maneuver narrow aisles as well as some other students, but she may certainly write as well or better. Rather than looking at students with impairments as wounded or ill, teachers need to see them in the same light as other non-traditional learners—in need of creative, carefully targeted methods to help each individual become the best possible writer.

Legal Issues in Teaching Students with Impairments

American citizens with physical or mental impairments have legal protection from discrimination based on section 504 of the Rehabilitation Act of 1973, the Individuals with Disabilities Education Act (IDEA) of 1975, and the Americans with Disabilities Act of 1990. This means that if they meet the basic entrance requirements, they are entitled to equal access and equal education in all public educational institutions. The Rehabilitation Act states that "no qualified handicapped person shall, solely on the basis of handicap, be excluded from participation in, be denied the benefits of, or otherwise subjected to discrimination under any program receiving or benefiting from Federal financial aid" (Latham & Latham, 39). IDEA assures that children with impairments receive a "free appropriate public education which emphasizes special education and related services to meet their unique needs" (Latham & Latham, 57). The Americans with Disabilities Act aims to end discrimination "against individuals with disabilities in the area of employment, education, public accommodations, and licensing of professional and other activities" (Latham & Latham, 75). In 1997, IDEA was reauthorized with a number of changes, mainly centered on the inclusion of parents in decision-making meetings. Another important change involved the recognition and inclusion of Attention Deficit Hyperactivity Disorder (ADHD) as one of the recognized disabilities (Education).

Although all of this legislation has benefited people with impairments, it has not ensured equal educational opportunity because, as in the case of separate but equal responses to racial segregation, no acceptable description of "equal education" exists for people with impairments.

In the last thirty years, the disability movement has sought and gained educational access for many of this nontraditional-student group. However, law does not legislate pedagogy, and there is no clear indication that teaching methods have changed to include and/or meet the needs of this diverse group of students. Because the type and degree of disability varies widely from one individual to another and because writing is itself a complex activity, writing teachers need an arsenal of complex and varied techniques to do an effective job teaching writing to students with impairments.

A Need for Change

Early approaches to educating students with impairments centered on special education classes taught by teachers trained to work with special-needs students. This "solution" isolated and marginalized young people, marking them as functionally disabled and unable to fit in with other learners. For this and other reasons, students with impairments have not been successful students. Statistics from a 1993 American Association of Disabled Persons report indicate that 48.9 million Americans, nearly one in five, had some type of impairment (McNeil). A 1997 U.S. Department of Education report "reveals that less than 50% of students with disabilities receive a regular diploma at graduation, and 38% drop out before graduation" (Wade and Zone, 7). Dismayed by these results and in an attempt to find a better system, educators today favor mainstreaming impaired students, keeping them in classrooms with same-age schoolmates and providing various types of accommodation to ensure their success. Like other nontraditional students, those with impairments need advocates. Bruggemann et al. argue that "disability is a category of oppression, a political status" (373). Learners with impairments may suffer the same sense of shame, frustration, and exclusion as those who feel different because of ethnicity, race, language, gender, or class. Teachers and administrators can join with parents to help alleviate these feelings and remove the false binary of able/disabled.

Any change must take into account the enormous variety among students with impairments. Approaches must be inexpensive, adaptable to individual needs, and easy to apply for a single student or group. For example, Giangreco and Doyle describe a multilevel instruction situation where "a student with disabilities and nondisabled peers participate together in a shared activity" (60) but with different outcome expectations. In this setting, students work together toward the same goal but are assessed according to ability-based rubrics. This general plan can work for any number of students with many different kinds of impairment. It is easy to implement, requiring only the creation of multiple rubrics.

Aids for the Physically Impaired

Accommodations for students with physical impairments probably create the greatest financial outlay, and administrators will often argue against purchasing special equipment if it promises to benefit only a few students. This response is understandable in a society that values the greatest good for the majority. Minority student advocates must attack such attitudes, however, through social activism and aggressive fundraising. Educators have a responsibility to find and tap available funding sources such as government and community grants.

Accommodations for students with physical impairments vary. In the writing classroom, students with visual problems may need computers with large monitors and/or large size print on produced copies of essays. Visually impaired students may also require Braille translations, textbook readers (human or mechanical), notetakers or tape recorders, and other devices to reduce the effects of impairment. Teachers should be aware of helpful hints like the ability to increase the size of computer-screen text in Microsoft Word by as much as 500%. One need only click the appropriate box on the right-hand side of the toolbar. A teacher who stops to think about the needs of visually impaired students will seek more tips like this one to offer class members. Of course, this kind of advice may serve a purpose for ALL students, not just those who have trouble seeing.

Hearing might not seem as important in the teaching of writing, but, in fact, hearing-impaired students may miss important instruction if they are not provided with notetakers (often typing notes onto a laptop computer that the student can read immediately) or signers. At the very least, writing teachers can provide printed copies of lessons, assignments, grading rubrics, etc. These devices also help students with ADD and any others with poor concentration or poor note-taking skills.

Wheelchair users need the seemingly obvious assistance of wide aisles and doors, accessible restroom facilities, and well-maintained elevators. While obvious, such accommodations are often unavailable or faulty. A schoolmate of mine seldom used the restroom because even the stall designed for wheelchairs was inappropriate for her type of impairment. Rather than a wide stall that allowed her chair to roll in next to the commode, she was expected to face her chair to the commode and somehow shift herself from one chair to another. Since this action was not possible, the best she could do was close the stall door and make use of a plastic jar that she then had to wash out in the public area and carry around among her belongings—a solution fraught with potential for embarrassment. Another wheelchair user at the same school habitually waited by the elevator before class for someone to ride up with her. If no one happened by, she was late to class. "I'm not a coward," she told me, "but I'm not stupid either." After spending an hour alone in a stuck elevator on two different occasions, unable to use the emergency telephone because it was placed well above her reach, she simply refused to take the chance again.

Money provides the key to helping the physically impaired, and teachers can prevent impairment from becoming disability by taking a firm stance. They need to voice their concerns and encourage appropriate spending to aid people with impairments. Even in a selfish society, this makes good sense because any citizen may be temporarily disabled and may need a safe elevator or an accessible toilet. Anyone who has ever broken a leg and been forced to maneuver around campus on crutches, been through a pregnancy, or been temporarily but severely ill can appreciate the value of such accommodations.

Dealing with Learning Disabilities

Probably the most difficult impairments for educators to deal with are the invisible ones. Often clumped together under the generic label of learning disabilities (LD), these include ADD, dyslexia, hyperactivity, and a wide range of cognitive difficulties caused by stroke, accident, or disease. An official definition of LD appears in Public Law 94-142, the Education for All Handicapped Children Act. It calls LD a "disorder in one or more of the basic psychological processes involved in understanding or using language, spoken or written, which may manifest itself in an imperfect ability to listen, think, speak, read, write, spell or do mathematical calculations" (Learning Disabilities). The law further states that "LD does not include learning problems that are primarily the result of visual, hearing or motor handicaps; mental retardation, or environmental, cultural, or economic disadvantage" (Learning Disabilities). Students with LD, approximately 2% to 3% of the general population in the United States (Learning Disabilities) usually seem perfectly normal and often get scolded by both teachers and parents who call them lazy or careless. Ironically, these so-called underachievers are often intelligent students who work harder than anyone else just to get by. If their impairment goes undiagnosed, their efforts go unrecognized. The outcome is frustration, failure, or both.

Unfortunately, no one plan helps all learning-disabled students. Every condition is different, and each individual's response to his or her impairment must be addressed. Dyslexia, for instance, is a lifelong condition "believed to stem from a neurophysiological flaw in the brain's ability to process language" (Corrigan, 155). This condition may, in various degrees, interfere with a student's ability to read effectively. Another student may have trouble dealing with the mechanics of writing. Others have difficulty remembering and following complicated directions, dividing complex tasks into their component parts or steps, or figuring out how to get from the kernel of an idea to finished product. Obviously these problems have a tremendous impact on students in writing classes. Undiagnosed dyslexia can convince learners that they are stupid and incapable of achieving even average levels of success. Dyslexics often end up relegated to classes for uncooperative or low I.Q. students where they receive none of the assistance that can help them overcome their disability. Once diagnosed, however, help is available.

Corrigan lists methods that aid dyslexic students in writing classrooms. Among his suggestions are weekly one-on-one conferences, instruction and grading of study skills, frequent classroom discussion of assigned readings, an emphasis on and grading of each step in the writing process, peer collaboration, and a general understanding by the teacher of the special needs associated with dyslexia. Corrigan, himself a dyslexic, reminds readers that this condition is not a disease; rather it is a disability that can be overcome with proper methodology and practice.

ADHD, recognized in 1997 as a form of LD, manifests itself in the students' inability "to sit still, plan ahead, finish tasks, or be fully aware of what's going on around them" (National). This condition, formerly known as hyperkinesis, "affects 3 to 5 percent of all children, perhaps as many as 2 million American children" (National). It appears more often in males. The condition "often continues into adolescence and adulthood" (National). To accommodate ADHD students in the classroom, experts recommend providing students with quiet work areas free from distraction. ADHD students need an area where they can move around freely and the kind of relaxed atmosphere that makes this movement possible. They also benefit from clearly posted rules and rewards for good behavior. They may need extra time for tests and regular review of instructions plus written copies of all directions for completing work (National).

As in the case of dyslexia and ADHD, most LDs can be surmounted, but only if teachers feel prepared to help. Surprisingly, most teachers are already better prepared than they know. Most of the practices suggested by experts are already within the scope of the average teacher, and these same tactics also help other students who may or may not have identified disabilities. All students may enjoy the opportunity to move around the classroom rather than remaining seated for the entire period. All can benefit from a designated quiet environment where they can focus without distraction. Teachers can easily build physical activity into lesson plans and can set aside quiet corners for focused study. Certain students may need extra time to complete a test or an assignment; the quiet corner can serve this purpose, too, or due dates can be staggered. If teachers contract due dates and grading rubrics with each student, special accommodations will not seem extraordinary and will not mark any student as having an impairment. Such change often costs nothing. As in the teaching of any non-traditional student, teachers can make a big difference merely by employing a wider range of already existing strategies, and perhaps using them more often with students who have diagnosed disabilities.

In addition, teachers can advise testing for students who seem to be struggling. A diagnosed impairment is much easier to deal with than one that is only suspected. Brueggemann et al. describe diagnosis as an epiphany for many disabled learners. They say, "Diagnosis initiates a transformation because when someone finds out that he has LD, he realizes that he is not stupid, limited, or lazy and thus is capable of learning" (374). Thus, teachers who worry about placing a stigma on a student by recommending tests do their students a disservice. Testing represents the first step toward freedom.

Using What We Know

As more students with impairments enter the mainstream of American education, outdated myths about the need for separation are giving way to new standards that stress inclusion and the ability of all teachers to teach all students. Giangreco and Doyle join other educators in arguing that teachers can improve instruction by adapting traditional methodology to the needs of a more varied audience. Furthermore, they can borrow techniques that have served special education for the benefit of a wide range of students with varying degrees of ability. Most of all, the new standards argue for an open attitude that recognizes the abilities of each individual and refuses to accept the able/disabled dichotomy (53–4).

Techniques discussed elsewhere in this book serve as well in instructing students with both physical and cognitive impairments. So do many of the standard practices of most teachers in the field. Giangreco and Doyle offer this list of methods to help students with impairments: "modeling and demonstration, class discussion, repeated exposure and practice, guided discovery, experiments, field study, participatory activities, use of multi-media technology, use of question-asking strategies, use of manipulative materials, educational games and play, use of positive and negative examples, corrective feedback, and individual or small-group projects" (64). Nothing on this list is new to the average teacher.

Collaborative learning, recommended for other nontraditional learners, is well suited to the integration of impaired students into regular activities. Students might, for example, work together on a research essay. Physically mobile team members can search the library stacks while a wheelchair-bound team member uses a computer to check Internet sources. A dyslexic student may listen to a teammate's summary of an article and then write a section of text that will later be edited by yet another member. By dividing labor into a series of tasks and assigning each task to the member with greatest skills in that area, the entire team can be productive and successful. In this kind of cooperative environment, students work together toward a common goal, each contributing according to ability and each challenged by other members to do his or her best work. In the process, learners come to accept difference and to value the person over the impairment.

I look forward to reading a new book by Patricia A. Dunn (due out in October, 2001) called *Talking, Sketching, Moving: Multiple Literacies in the Teaching of Writing.* By calling on multiple ways of learning, Dunn argues against too much reliance on linguistic pathways and suggests other ways of teaching students to write. Too often writing teachers get stuck in methodologies that have proven successful for traditional students and forget to try new approaches that will be equally successful for prototypical learners and perhaps more successful for the nontraditional learners in their classes. We who teach writing need to explore every possible avenue for improving pedagogy, and it seems to me that Dunn offers interesting possibilities.

In a more generalized approach, Wade and Zone promote what they call scaffolded instruction (14). Designed to benefit all nontraditional students, this method is accomplished by a continuous assessment of students' abilities. The teacher provides plenty of support for challenging tasks and then allows students to guide themselves as their skills increase. Guidance takes the form of "modeling, demonstrating, explaining, questioning, and directing" (14). Explicit instruction is recommended for new, difficult activities, and teachers are encouraged to engage in *think-alouds*, during which they model and explain "both the overt procedures of the strategy and the covert thinking processes that are involved" (14). Rather than turning think-alouds into a lecture situation, they should take the form of collaborative discussions where students share what they know and make suggestions about content and procedures. As students demonstrate proficiency with designated tasks, the teacher takes on the role of coach or facilitator, and students exercise greater control over activities. This process gives students with and without impairments the structure they need, the challenge they enjoy, and ever-increasing degrees of autonomy.

Wade and Zone also recommend alternative assessment as a means to help impaired students achieve success in the classroom (16–17). In their critique of standardized achievement tests, the authors argue that standardized assessment devices "serve to legitimize the 'disabling' of minority students by locating the problem or deficiency in the student rather than in school practices that are disempowering" (17). Instead,   educators need to use performance-based assessment wherein students are evaluated on how well they think and solve problems in their own cultural and physical environments. Obviously, social and political action must be employed to change notions about what is standard for today's students.

Normalcy is, in fact, socially defined, and society can change. No longer can we expect all students to look, think, dress, act, and learn alike. Our world is too diverse, too multifaceted. This lesson has not reached all citizens, but teachers can help to spread the word. We can do this by making difference a topic of discussion, including the difference caused by impairment. As Bruggemann suggests, we must make disability visible to students (382). Once they have thought and talked about what it means to have an impairment, they will more easily come to accept it as just one more kind of difference, like the difference between Christian and Jew or the difference between one ethnicity and another. The common reaction of parents when their children see someone with an impairment is to tell them to be quiet. "Don't stare," they say. "It's not polite to ask questions." In spite of their very good intentions, their unwillingness to embarrass the person with the impairment, these parents inadvertently teach their children that an impairment is an embarrassing abnormality, a hush-hush situation that they should shy away from. Thus, they continue the attitudes that turn impairment into disability. Educators have a responsibility to change these notions, to open up discussion and to confront unacknowledged fear and prejudice.

Reducing Stress

According to one report, "school related stress is the most prevalent, untreated cause of academic failure in our schools" (Rubenzer). This problem affects many students but has particularly negative results for those with impairments. Even students with histories of classroom success worry about assignments and tests. It is not surprising, then, that the pressure to do well on difficult tasks can trigger anxiety, fear, and frustration in learners who have previously experienced failure. To complicate matters, stress itself can hinder performance by causing students to rush through work, to doubt the correctness of their responses, to become distracted, or even to suffer panic or anxiety attacks that virtually paralyze them.

A number of approaches exist for reducing stress in the classroom. These include fostering a relaxed atmosphere, providing humorous outlets, practicing relaxation techniques, and including problems and questions within the comfort zone of all students as well as other problems that challenge them (Rubenzer). Providing relaxing periods with restful activities, perhaps including soft music and dim lights, can help teachers, too, who also operate under stress. In writing classes, these rest periods can accompany freewriting or journaling activities, or the teacher can play tapes of authors reading their work. An occasional video of a literary work can inspire young writers as can the showing of restful slides like seascapes or sunsets. In addition to reducing stress, such activities help students think of writing as a pleasurable event rather than a time of stress.

Teachers of students with impairments have a responsibility to plan ahead, to be flexible, and to enlist outside support. Much ink has been spent on the debate about the teacher's role as activist, but a teacher does not have to be a radical to understand that teaching is never only about what goes on inside the classroom. Teachers can also try to discover what their students need on campus outside the classroom doors as well as what they need at home and in the community. Educators can provide answers to questions beyond the prescribed lesson. Education has long aimed to create good citizens. I believe the best citizen maintains an open attitude toward differences of all kinds, including differences caused by physical and mental impairments. Some of the responsible educators' goals must focus on helping students recognize the value in every other student. They can do this by modeling open attitudes and by accommodating the various needs of all students in their classrooms.

Call for Further Research

Too little research focuses on the problems of impaired students and the disability created by their conditions. I hope that readers of this book will recognize the value of such research, will report on their own experiences and those of their students, and will work to create new catalysts for learning that serve all students, not just the ideal students who exist only in our imaginations.

Benefits of a Nondisabling Society for ALL Citizens

Inclusive education benefits students with impairments and all other non-traditional students as well. As Wade and Zone make clear, "advocates of inclusion seek to change the philosophy and structure of schools so that *all* students, despite differences in language, culture, ethnicity, economic status, gender, and ability, can be educated with their peers in the regular classroom in their neighborhood schools" (7). These are goals we should all consider as we prepare lessons for the multiple needs of our students.

WORKS CITED

Brueggemann, Brenda Jo; Linda Fedlmeier White, Patricia A. Dunn, Barbara A. Heifferon, & Johnson Cheu. "Becoming Visible: Lessons in Disability." *College Composition and Communication*, 57.3, 368–98, February 2001..

Corrigan, John. "Teaching Writing to Dyslexic Students: A Guide for the Composition Instructor." In Richard L. Graves (Ed.). *Writing, Teaching, Learning: A Sourcebook.* Portsmouth, NH: Boynton/Cook, 1999.

Dunn, Patricia A. *Talking, Sketching, Moving: Multiple Literacies in the Teaching of Writing.* Portsmouth, NH: Boynton/Cook, 2001.

Education Development Center. "The Individuals with Disabilities Education Act Amendments of 1997." *http://www.ideapractices.org /lawandregs.htm.* 9/19/01

Giangreco, Michael F. & Mary Beth Doyle. "Curricular and Instructional Considerations for Teaching Students with Disabilities in General Education Classrooms." In Wade, 51–69.

Kelman, Mark & Gillian Lester. *Jumping the Queue: An Inquiry into the Legal Treatment of Students with Learning Disabilities.* Cambridge, MA: Harvard University, 1997.

Latham, Peter S. & Patricia H. Latham. *Learning Disabilities and the Law.* Washington, DC: JKL Communications, 1993.

"Learning Disabilities." ERIC Digest #407. Revised. Reston, VA: ERIC Clearinghouse on the Handicapped and Gifted Children, 1986.

McNeil, J. M. "Americans with Disabilities: 1991–92. Washington, DC: U.S. Bureau of the Census Current Population Report, 1993.

National Institute of Mental Health. "Attention Deficit Hyperactivity Disorder." *http://www.nimh.gov/publicat/adhd.cfm.* 9/14/01.

Rubenzer, Ronald L. "Stress Management for the Learning Disabled." ERIC Digest #452, 1988.

Sullivan, Martin. "Does it say what we mean, do we mean what it says, do we know what we are saying? Assessing Disability Policy in Tertiary Institutions from a Social Model Perspective." *http://www.bath.ac.uk/ Students/learningsupport/webb/sullivan.htm.* 6/16/2001.

Teaching Students With Disabilities 2.2 Horsham, PA: LRP Publications, 2001.

Wade, Suzanne (Ed.). *Inclusive Education: A Casebook and Readings for Prospective and Practicing Teachers.* Mahwah, NJ: Lawrence Erlbaum, 2000.

Wade, Suzanne & Judy Zone. "Creating Inclusive Classrooms: An Overview." In Wade, 3–27.

"Working Together: Faculty and Students with Disabilities." University of Washington DO-IT Resources. *http://www.washington.edu/doit/ brochures/Academics/teachers.html* 6/16/2001.

LAST WORD

The student population of American schools has changed drastically in recent decades. Pedagogy has not always kept pace, and today's teachers in writing classes, and in general, often use traditional methodology to teach nontraditional students. This book suggests an open-minded look at unconventional techniques and a reworking of the conventional to meet the needs of a new world of writers.

Teaching in the twenty-first century and beyond requires an understanding of and direct confrontation with difference. The old values of equal education to create good citizens in a homogeneous state do not apply. We now face students of diverse color, home language, culture, and ability, and it is our responsibility as educators to provide the best possible education for all. The best is not the same in all cases, so we have to add to our teaching repertoire. Instead of teaching for consensus, we can encourage a dialogue of difference that allows individuals to hold opinions unlike their classmates and still feel like a part of a learning community. We can use a wide range of techniques and lessons, and learn to accept diverse responses to our prompts. We can value each student's home language and, without judging one over the other, introduce another language—the academic—and help students know when to use each.

None of this will happen quickly or easily. Systems resist change, and innovation may receive negative responses from students, parents, other teachers, and administrators. Nevertheless, teachers must persevere in their efforts to affect change. Working quietly within the system, we can behave in subversive ways, slipping in new methods and new attitudes that must eventually take hold and be replicated. They will be replicated because they will inevitably bring about positive results. An open, caring teaching and learning community can infect others. This is the place to begin. This is the time.

INDEX

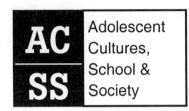

Adolescent Cultures, School & Society

Joseph L. DeVitis & Linda Irwin-DeVitis
GENERAL EDITORS

As schools struggle to redefine and restructure themselves, they need to be cognizant of the new realities of adolescents. Thus, this series of monographs and textbooks is committed to depicting the variety of adolescent cultures that exist in today's post-industrial societies. It is intended to be a primarily qualitative research, practice, and policy series devoted to contextual interpretation and analysis that encompasses a broad range of interdisciplinary critique. In addition, this series will seek to provide a pragmatic, pro-active response to the current backlash of conservatism that continues to dominate political discourse, practice, and policy. This series seeks to address issues of curriculum theory and practice; multicultural education; aggression and violence; the media and arts; school dropouts; homeless and runaway youth; alienated youth; at-risk adolescent populations; family structures and parental involvement; and race, ethnicity, class, and gender studies.

Send proposals and manuscripts to the general editors at:

Joseph L. DeVitis & Linda Irwin-DeVitis
College of Education and Human Development
University of Louisville
Louisville, KY 40292-0001

To order other books in this series, please contact our Customer Service Department at:

(800) 770-LANG (within the U.S.)
(212) 647-7706 (outside the U.S.)
(212) 647-7707 FAX

or browse online by series at:

WWW.PETERLANGUSA.COM